What's with My Body?

The Girls' Book of Answers to Growing Up, Looking Good, and Feeling Great

Selene Yeager

Prima Publishing

Published by Prima Publishing, Roseville, California. Member of the Crown Publishing Group, a division of Random House, Inc.

PRIMA PUBLISHING and colophon are trademarks of Random House, Inc., registered with the United States Patent and Trademark Office.

Interior design by Melanie Haage.
Interior illustrations by Laurie Baker-McNeile.

Library of Congress Cataloging-in-Publication Data
Yeager, Selene.
What's with my body? : the girls' book of answers
to growing up, looking good, and feeling great / Selene Yeager.
p.   cm.
Includes index.
ISBN 0-7615-3723-6
1. Teenage girls—Growth. 2. Teenage girls—Physiology.
3. Teenage girls—Health and hygiene. 4. Sex instruction for girls. I. Title.
RJ144.Y43   2002
613.9'04243--dc21   2002070380

02 03 04 05 06 HH 10 9 8 7 6 5 4 3 2 1
Printed in the United States of America

First Edition

Visit us online at www.primapublishing.com

For Juniper.
May you grow up happy, healthy, and strong.

Contents

Acknowledgments

Thanks to my husband, Dave, for his undying support; the great girls who breathed life into the text: Samantha, Britany, Ashlyn, Julie, Melissa, Chris, Christie, Liz, Tara, and Kortni; and to Michelle, Denise, and Alice for giving me the opportunity to work on this important (yet fun) project, and for their support in bringing it through to fruition.

Introduction

If you're reading this book, you're going through one of the most exciting, confusing, and ever-changing times of your life. Almost every day you wake up, you're facing something new. Your feet have grown. You notice hair where you never had it before. Suddenly you're stressing about tampons and pads. It's a lot to handle, and though the adults in your life are there to help, it's not always easy for you to ask questions—or for them to give you all the answers you need. (Remember, it's been a long time since they went through puberty!) That's where this book comes in.

We've taken hundreds of the most commonly asked questions from girls just like you and have gone straight to the best experts in the country to get no-nonsense answers. No question was too embarrassing and every answer is direct, with subjects ranging from your first period and sexual development to tattoos and piercings. You name it, we've covered it. This book isn't designed to replace the important adults in your life, of course, but rather to give you a little education so all these sensitive, tricky topics are easier to talk about.

And about those adults in your life: You'll notice that we talk a lot about parents and "mom and dad," like when we suggest you talk to mom and dad before running off to get your tongue pierced. We recognize, of course, that not everyone has both their biological parents at home, and that families come in all shapes and sizes, with stepmoms and stepdads, aunts and uncles, godparents, foster parents, older siblings, grandparents, and single parents. When we refer to your family, we mean any important adult you have in your life at home. Now, on with the book! And best of luck on your journey growing up!

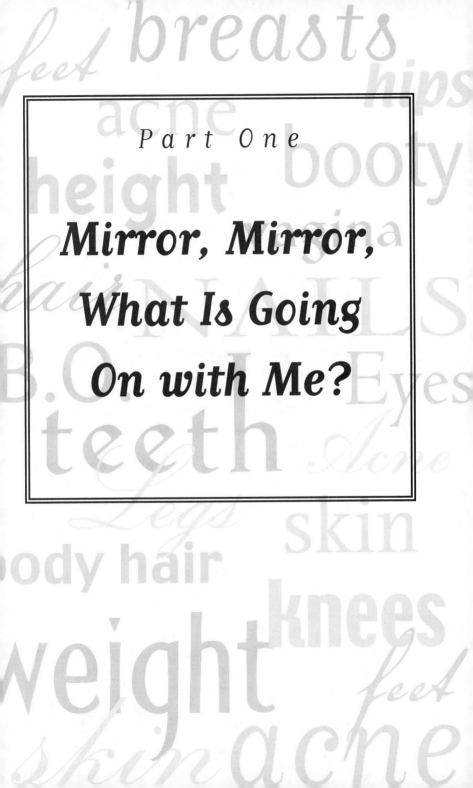

Part One

Mirror, Mirror, What Is Going On with Me?

Acne

Face the World with a Smile!

When it comes to zits, there's one thing you have to know: Though you feel totally alone with your blemishes, everyone and her sister gets them. Almost 100 percent of teens and preteens will sprout blackheads and pimples at this time of life. But just because you've hit puberty doesn't mean you can't put your best face forward! That same increase in oils that can contribute to pimples also gives your complexion a healthy shimmer and a rosy glow. Here are the answers you need for keeping your face clean, clear, and healthy.

> "I haven't noticed any pimples yet."
>
> **Samantha, 9**

Q. What is acne anyway?

A. Acne is an umbrella term doctors use for skin problems caused by clogged or inflamed pores. Lean your face way close to a mirror and you'll see the tiny holes we call pores—the opening to hair follicles. You have pores all over your body. Some have hair growing out of them; others obviously don't. Below the surface where you can't see, these pores contain sebaceous (pronounced "se-BAY-shis") glands, which produce an oil called sebum ("SEE-bum") that keeps your skin and hair moist and healthy. Sebum also carries away dead skin cells from inside your pores. Sebaceous glands are especially concentrated on your face, neck, chest, and back—not coincidentally, where acne strikes most often! When pores become blocked with oil and dead skin cells, you get one of three types of acne:

1. **Blackheads.** Those black dots that appear on your nose, cheeks, and chin are called blackheads. It looks like you could just scrub them off but don't try—not even sandpaper would work. They're actually pores that are clogged and swollen with oil and dead skin cells. The pigment in the oil makes it look black in there.

2. **Whiteheads.** Like blackheads, whiteheads are clogged, swollen pores. Except in the case of whiteheads, dead skin cells have clumped together and blocked the surface of the pore, forming a small white spot.

3. **Pimple.** Pimples are the sore red bumps, often with a white tip, we all dread. Pimples happen when normal bacteria from your skin get into your already-clogged pores and start multiplying like bunnies. Infection-fighting white blood cells flood the area to fight the bacteria, and you end up with a painful, pus-filled zit. Sometimes the follicle becomes so inflamed that its walls burst, spilling this facial waste under the surrounding skin. That causes firm, deep red bumps and swellings called cysts or nodules—the most severe kind of acne.

Q. Why do I suddenly have acne now?

A. Puberty, baby. Your body pumps out mega-amounts of hormones to help you grow breasts and become capable of having babies. Along with the flood of female hormones are some predominantly male hormones, like androgens. Androgens stimulate oil production, so your sebaceous glands, which have been functioning just fine until recently, are now gushing like miniature oil wells. All that oil combined with the dead skin cells you're shedding sets the stage for plenty of pimples. And if your mom or dad had bad acne when they were your age, you might too, because acne can run in families. You might also notice that your breakouts happen more before your period. That's because your body produces more oil-stimulating hormones during that time.

"I just started getting a few pimples, but not too many. I am very fortunate. My mom told me she would take me to a dermatologist if it gets bad and I need help getting rid of them. Right now, I just wash my face more to keep them away."

Britany, 11

Q. Do potato chips and Hershey's Kisses cause acne?

A. Truth is, nobody really knows. Doctors have tried to find a link between acne and certain foods like fried foods and chocolate for years, but they haven't proved any connections. What they do know is that your body works its all-around best when you're eating mostly healthy foods instead of greasy junk and candy bars. So cleaning up your diet with more fruits, vegetables, and grains may help clean up your complexion, too. Also, everybody responds differently to certain foods, so pay attention to how your skin reacts. If chips or chocolate seem to prompt your pimples, cut back.

Q. Why do I always get a pimple just when I want to look my best?!

A. It does seem like school pictures cause pimples, but they don't. It's the stress that you feel around important events that can contribute to breakouts. When you're stressed out, you produce more androgens, which, as you already know, leads to more oil and gunked-up pores. Instead of bugging out about a big party or the first day in a new grade, take all that energy and do something positive with it. The same is true for big exams and other stressful events. Go for a bike ride, play some soccer with your girlfriends, toss some sandwiches in your backpack and have a picnic in the park. However you do it, be sure to take time to blow off your stress. You don't need pimples making your life more miserable.

Q. Will I ever outgrow this?

A. Most likely. Acne usually settles down by the time you graduate from high school. But since your hormones go through changes all your life, the occasional breakout is common, even in adults. The important thing is to know how to take care of your skin to limit breakouts. Also, there are many good medications today that treat and prevent pimples. A lot of them are available at the drug store. Some, for the more serious cases, are prescribed by your dermatologist. So you see, you don't have to sit around waiting for acne to run its course.

"I wash my face every night before bed.
It's part of my daily schedule."

Ashlyn, 13

Q. How can I prevent zits?

A. Keeping your skin clean is priority one. That doesn't mean scrubbing, rubbing, and washing ten times a day—that stuff can make acne worse. Rather, wash your face twice a day with a gentle cleanser. Here are some specific recommendations:

- **If you have oily skin.** Look for a liquid cleanser that contains salicylic acid. It helps empty out blackheads and whiteheads, cut down on the oiliness of your skin, and keep your pores clear.

- **If you have drier, more sensitive skin.** Try a gentle, non-soap cleanser like Cetaphil. It cleans pores without removing the oil you need. Also, skip the washcloth and use clean hands instead, since washcloths can trap bacteria and contribute to breakouts in sensitive skin.

- **If your skin is neither oily nor dry, but you still suffer an occasional breakout.** Any gentle cleanser will work.

These are some other pimple-preventing steps you can take:

- **Wear funky hair clips, ties, and barrettes.** Oil from your hair may contribute to oil on your face, making forehead breakouts worse. Play around with hairstyles that keep your hair from hanging heavy on your face.

- **Pop the pillowcase in the wash.** Acne-causing bacteria can build up on pillowcases and sheets. Clean them both once a week.

- **Keep a hands-off policy.** Touching your face adds bacteria and spreads it around.

- **Choose makeup carefully.** Makeup, moisturizers, and even hair gel can contribute to clogged pores. Make sure any product you use around your face says *noncomedogenic* or *nonacnegenic* on the label. That means it won't cause zits.

Q. How can I get rid of zits?

A. You often can treat acne yourself with products from the drugstore. Try one of these:

- **Benzoyl peroxide.** Many over-the-counter acne treatments contain benzoyl peroxide—a classic in acne care. It fights bacteria and clears blocked follicles. Be sure to follow the directions on the label. Test it on a small patch of skin first, to be sure you're not allergic. And don't get it on your clothes—it bleaches.

- **Salicylic acid.** The same washes that prevent blackheads and whiteheads (see "How can I prevent zits?" page 5) can help clear them up.

For more stubborn acne, a dermatologist can recommend one of these stronger solutions:

- **Tretinoin (Retin-A).** Products that contain chemicals called retinols can help treat acne by speeding up how quickly your skin regenerates so you have less build-up in your pores. Retin-A can be irritating to sensitive skin and it leaves you much more vulnerable to sunlight, so it's not for everyone.

- **Oral meds.** Depending on your acne, a dermatologist may prescribe pills for you to take that can treat your acne from the inside out. These include hormones and antibiotics. Because these medications are strong and can have serious side effects, it's very important that you follow the doctor's instructions very carefully and that you speak up about any problems right away. Also, be patient. These treatments can take a few months to kick in.

No matter how you get rid of them, pimples often leave behind what is called a post-inflammatory erythema—little red spots that seem to take *forever* to go away. It can actually take six to twelve months for them to fade completely on their own. If you want to speed up the process, try a fading cream that contains glycolic acid.

Leave Your Face Alone!!!

The temptation may feel overwhelming, but resist the urge to squeeze, pop, or pick at your pimples. Yes, everyone pops pimples sometimes, and it usually ends up okay, but you take a risk of making your acne worse every time you do. Squeezing pimples can drive the oil and bacteria deeper into your skin, leading to a bigger infection. Picking, popping, and scratching can also leave permanent scars.

If you have severe acne (many pimples and cysts) that isn't responding to basic care, keep your hands away from your face and talk to your mom and dad about seeing a dermatologist to help prevent the scarring this type of acne can create.

Check It Out!

American Academy of Dermatology (AAD)
930 North Meacham Road
P.O. Box 4014
Schaumburg, Illinois 60168-4014
Phone: (847) 330-0230
Web site: www.aad.org (they even have a cool link called
"Kid's Connection" for preteens and adolescents)

Breasts

Sprouting a New Shape

Of all the changes that happen with puberty, growing breasts is probably the most noticeable—to you *and* to the world around you. Some girls are thrilled at the first sign of budding breasts; others feel slightly embarrassed or shy. It's natural to feel a whole bunch of emotions as you watch your body change before your eyes—especially since you don't have any control over it! It's also natural to have a ton of questions, like "How big will I be?" "What if my breasts are lopsided?" "Do I need a bra?" And so on and so on and so on. Here are the answers to your "developing" questions.

Q. When should my breasts start to grow?

A. There's no magical age when your breasts begin to sprout. Most girls will notice changes sometime between ages nine and twelve, though it's normal to start a little earlier or a little later. For many girls, sprouting breasts are the first sign of puberty that they can actually see, even though their hormones may have been busy working for a while already. And some girls notice changes happening before their breasts start growing, changes in underarm hair or pubic hair. Or it may seem to be happening all at once!

9

Breasts begin growing when your body starts producing more of the female hormone estrogen (see Hormones, page 100). Estrogen tells your body that it's time to start developing breast buds, which contain fat, other tissues, and milk glands, which, when it's time to feed a baby, produce milk that it sends through ducts in your nipples. Your body pads these important glands and ducts with a cushion of fat. Of course, this doesn't happen overnight! Your breasts develop in five stages, which usually take about five years to complete, though some girls go through the stages superfast, while others take more time.

- **Stage 1:** Stage 1 is kind of a fakeout. Your breasts are still flat, but your nipples are a little raised. And the areola (the dark area around the nipple) is small. Inside, though, your ovaries may be getting the message from your brain, the ol' pituitary gland (the gland in the brain that sets almost all of puberty in motion, see Hormones, page 100), that it's time to start pumping out estrogen, which will send your breasts into stage 2.

- **Stage 2:** Breast buds form! Under your nipples, you'll notice a raised bump that causes your nipples to stick out from your chest. These buds contain all the stuff that will eventually create your breasts, including milk glands and fat tissue. Your nipples and areolas will get larger and maybe a little darker. Don't panic if these buds don't form at the same time. It's normal for one to get a little head start on the other.

- **Stage 3:** With your body cushioning the area with more fat tissue, your breasts continue to grow. They may look a little pointy as they develop outward. Your nipples and areolas continue to get larger and darker. This is when some girls consider wearing a bra.

- **Stage 4:** In this stage, your nipples and areolas continue to grow and form a little mound at the end of your breasts. Some girls go through this stage. Some don't.

- **Stage 5:** Congratulations, your breasts are fully developed. By stage 5, breasts are rounder and fuller. The areolas are blended into the breasts, and the nipples are raised at the tips of your breasts. Though your breasts will continue to change during adulthood— during pregnancy, when your body weight changes, when you go through normal hormonal shifts—basically, what you see in this final stage is the size and shape of your adult breasts.

Q. My breasts hurt sometimes. Is this normal?

A. It's completely normal for breasts to be tender and ache or hurt a little when they first start to form (stage 2). It's also common for your breasts to feel a little tender around your menstrual cycle, especially before your period. Of course, if you have lots of pain and it seems to come at weird times—not related to your period—it's a good idea to have your mom make an appointment with your doctor to make sure everything's okay.

Q. Is there anything I can do to make my breasts grow faster or get bigger?

A. You could get down on the floor and start doing push-ups while chanting "We must. We must. We must increase our bust. The bigger the better, the tighter the sweater. We must. We must. We must increase our bust!" But that wouldn't do anything but make you feel silly. Seriously, years back, girls used to do all kinds of exercises to try to increase their breast size. But none of them really work. Exercises like push-ups are good for building up the muscles that lie underneath your breasts, so your breast may look *slightly* bigger. But since your breasts are made of fat tissue and glands, these exercises don't actually increase your breast size.

Likewise, you'll see all kinds of advertisements for wacky products, like breast enhancement creams that promise to give you big, voluptuous breasts. Don't buy it. No creams, potions, pills, or exercises will change the size and shape of your breasts. And you know what? That's okay. Your breasts will grow at the rate that's right for your body. And breasts of all sizes are beautiful. Even some models and actresses who got surgical breast implants to make their breasts bigger have had them removed in recent years, deciding that natural, normal-sized breasts really do look better.

Q. One of my breasts is bigger than the other. Will I be lopsided forever?

A. Don't worry! Chances are you won't be. It's very common for one breast to start developing even six months to a year before the other one. By the time you finish developing, both breasts are usually about the same shape and size. Remember, though, we're not perfectly symmetrical. If you hold your hands next to each other, you'll likely find that there are slight differences between the two. The same is true for your breasts. It's perfectly normal and natural for one to be slightly bigger than the other, or different in some other way. That said, sometimes a girl does end up with one breast that's considerably larger than the other. If it's troubling you, try wearing a slightly padded bra that will make you look more uniform.

Q. I have large breasts and boys at school make fun of me. What can I do?

A. This is definitely one of the worst parts about developing. Because your breasts are out there for the world to see, rude people—often boys—feel like they have the right to comment on them. Girls with large breasts can suffer the worst of this kind of harassment. Boys, and even some men, may stare, whistle, or make comments. First, don't feel bad about your body. It's developing in a natural way. Lots of girls and women have large breasts. Second, remember that you're more than a body. You're a complete, active girl who has tons of interests, talents, and hobbies that have zero to do with your cup size. Wear clothes you feel comfortable and confident in and hold your head up high. If the worst of the teasing is a few random comments, you can probably put an end to them by just ignoring the boy or telling him to stop. If the comments are constant, if you feel threatened, or if some guy starts grabbing at you (this happens more often than you realize), tell your parents or a teacher or counselor right away. This is sexual harassment and you don't have to take it, especially when you're at school. Unfortunately, there may be other circumstances where there's little you can do about rude remarks or stares. If you're walking down the street and a bunch of boys shout from a car or a man stares at you in a store, the best you can do is to ignore it and get out of that situation as fast as possible. While it may be tempting to yell back or say something rude in return, it could only make the situation worse, and it's not worth it. In the unlikely event that a stranger touches you, however, tell your parents *and* the police. Your body is yours alone *and* that's against the law.

"I've noticed that girls in my grade are developing at different rates. Most of my friends are more developed than me, but there are a few who haven't started developing very much yet. It can be a little weird."

Liz, 13

Q. I'm very flat-chested. I'm worried I'll never have breasts. Should I get a padded bra?

A. First, remember that some girls develop later than others. Some girls don't even really *start* developing until they're thirteen or fourteen years old. So even if you don't have the slightest bumps under your tank tops yet, don't freak. There's still time. Sure, it's also possible that your breasts will be smaller than some of your friends when they do develop. But that's okay, too. You don't need "big boobs" to be attractive. And if you're worried about boys, don't. Just like girls like all kinds of guys—tall, stocky, muscular, skinny—guys like all kinds of girls. And your breasts will probably look just right for your body. As far as getting a padded bra, a lightly padded bra may make you feel fuller. And if that makes you feel happier, that's okay too. But never forget that whether they're the size of peaches, melons, or cherries, those bulges on your chest are only a small part of who you really are. Don't be breast obsessed!

Q. My nipples stick in instead of out. Is something wrong with me?

A. Probably not. Some nipples appear to be sucked into their breasts. They're called *inverted* nipples, and they're perfectly normal. Sometimes, as a girl's breasts develop, inverted nipples will pop their heads out and stay out. Other times, they stay hidden. Women with inverted nipples have completely healthy breasts and can breast feed just like any other woman. It's important to keep inverted nipples clean, however, since they can be prone to infection. Ask your mom (she may have inverted nipples, too) or a doctor or nurse the best way to clean them. The only time to get an inverted nipple checked is if one or both become inverted sometime after puberty when your breasts are fully developed. Chances are, nothing is wrong. But nipples that invert out of the blue (again, once you're done developing) could be a sign of a medical condition, so it's best to get them checked.

Q. My breasts are very lumpy. Should I be worried?

A. With all the warnings girls hear about breast cancer, it's easy to spaz when you feel lumps in your breasts. But relax. First, though it *could* happen, breast cancer is *extremely rare,* if not unheard of, in teenagers and preteens. It's very common for breasts to feel lumpy as they sprout breast buds and begin to develop. It's also very common for girls and women to simply have lumpy breast tissue, technically called *fibrocystic* breasts. Women with fibrocystic breasts may notice that their breasts feel lumpier at certain times of the month—like before their periods—and they may be a little more tender. No matter what kind of breasts you have, lumpy or smooth, the important thing to do is to get in the habit of checking your breasts each month (see Start Self-Checking Today, page 17) so you know what your breasts feel like normally. Then, if you find a *new* lump or some other change, you can talk to your doctor about it.

Q. Will getting hit in the chest hurt my breasts?

A. No. Girls used to stress out that getting hit in the breasts would cause cancer or make them burst or some other catastrophe. But don't panic if an ill-aimed soccer ball slams into your sports bra. It may not feel great, but your breasts will bounce back just fine!

Q. I had fluid come out of my nipples the other day and it freaked me out! What is it?

A. Your breasts naturally produce some fluids, and it's not a cause for concern if occasionally a little comes out, especially if you've squeezed your nipples. The fluid that comes out, called *discharge,* is usually clear, cream-colored, or yellowish. You may also notice just a crust around the nipple from where some discharge came out and dried. This kind of nipple discharge is usually completely normal. But nipple discharge *can* be a sign of a medical condition, so it's still a good idea to get it checked by a doctor, just to make sure nothing's wrong.

Q. Sometimes my nipples get hard and stick out, and everyone can see them through my clothes. How can I stop this from happening?

A. This happens to *everybody* at some time or another. Nipples are very sensitive to stimulation. So if they get cold or your shirt rubs against them just right, they'll tighten up and get stiff and erect. They can also get erect seemingly out of nowhere, or even if you just have some sexy thoughts. So you can't really keep it from happening. What you can do, if it really stresses

Breasts

you out, is try buying bras with thicker cups so your nipples will be less prominent when they stand to attention. Otherwise, try not to bug out about it too much. Everyone, including boys, have nipples. And it's perfectly normal for them to be noticeable once in a while.

Q. If breasts are for feeding babies, will milk come out if I squeeze them?

A. Good question! The answer is, you only produce milk when you need it. The body is a pretty smart machine, and it doesn't like to waste energy. It doesn't bother making milk for years and years, when you're not going to use it. Instead, it waits until a baby is born to start producing the hormones that tell your milk glands it's time to fill up and get ready to deliver mom's milk to her newborn baby.

"I've just started getting breasts, but they're still pretty small. I wouldn't mind if they got a little bigger."

Julie, 11

Q. Will jogging make my breasts sag?

A. Most sagging, which occurs later in a woman's life, is the result of tissue changes that happen in our breasts as we age—not from letting our breasts bounce. That said, a lifetime of running without a bra could probably contribute to sagging. But if you wear a sports bra (a special, snug top that holds your breasts in place) while you run and play, sagging shouldn't be a concern—plus, it's a whole lot more comfortable not to have your breasts bouncing around!

For more on taking care of your breasts, see Bras, page 161.

Start Self-Checking Today!

Though you certainly don't need to stress about breast cancer now, it's important to start performing a monthly breast self-examination (BSE) while you're young so you know what your breasts feel like normally and so it's a regular habit when you're older and detecting breast cancer becomes more of a concern. Perform a BSE after your period each month (when your breasts are less tender). Here's what to do:

- **Look.** Stand topless in front of a mirror. Take a look at each breast. Notice size, shape, and skin color as well as the direction your nipples point. Raise your arms over your head and look at them again, making note of the same things. Check out your breasts from both sides as well as the front. Finally, put your hands on your hips and push your shoulders forward. Again, look at how your breasts hang and how they're shaped. You want to be alert for any changes in shape, size, or skin color and for any bumps or lumps around the contours of your breasts.

- **Feel.** Using the right hand for the left breast (and the left hand for the right breast), you now want to feel your breasts for any strange bumps or lumps (it helps to put a little lotion on your fingertips; you can also do this when you're soapy and slippery in the shower). Start up by your collarbone. Press firmly with your fingertips and rub in small circles, going back and forth across the entire chest area, working your way down your breast, being sure to check the entire breast, including the nipple area and the side of your breast under your arm. Do the same thing with the other breast. Now lie down (you probably wouldn't want to do this part in the shower) and do the feeling exam all over again on both breasts.

(continues on page 18)

(continued)

Now is also the time to start developing breast-healthy habits. There's plenty of stuff you can do while you're young to help help prevent cancer when you're older. Follow these tips to help protect your breasts:

- **Eat fruits and veggies.** Eating a healthful diet is good for your breasts and may actually fend off cancer later in life. Aim for five servings a day (see Nutrition, page 208).

- **Don't drink alcohol.** Alcohol raises your risk for breast cancer. In fact, there are a *lot* of reasons to steer clear of alcohol— especially when you're in your teens. And even once you're older, it's a good idea to limit your drinking to once in a while.

- **Exercise!** Regular exercise, like playing soccer, swimming, cycling, and whatever other activities you find fun, can protect your breasts and help keep them healthy.

Check It Out!

Susan G. Komen Breast Cancer Foundation
5005 LBJ Freeway
Suite 250
Dallas, Texas 75244
Phone: (972) 855-1600
Web site: www.breastcancerinfo.com (all kinds of info on breast care)

Body Hair

The Buzz on That New Fuzz

Many girls welcome the new breasts and few extra inches in height that come with puberty. But fewer are as happy with one of the other telltale signs of growing up—body hair. Sometime between the ages of eight and fourteen, you'll begin to notice hair cropping up where you once were bald. For some girls, underarm hair is the first sign of all the big changes yet to come. For others, it's the last development before they get their first period. Of course, under your arms isn't the only place new hair appears. New hair will likely show up on your arms, legs, pubic area, and face—particularly your upper lip and the back of your cheeks. It also can show up in places you never imagined, like around your nipples, on top of your feet, and even on your belly!

When you're not expecting it, this outgrowth of fuzz can be kind of startling. But it's perfectly normal. Here are answers to your most perplexing questions on body hair.

"I have some friends who have to shave their legs. But I don't have to do that yet, which is good."

Kortni, 10

Q. What is all this hair for anyway?

A. Unlike other animals, we don't need our body hair to protect us or keep us warm. But it does do some pretty cool things. For one, it makes your skin more sensitive to the touch, since brushing against the hair triggers nerves in your skin. So you can feel the slightest breeze or movement in the air. Believe it or not, body hair also may be one of nature's primitive ways of helping us attract the opposite sex. The same hormones that turn you from girl to woman are the ones responsible for body hair. Though it may at times seem weird and unattractive, body hair is just a part of who we are, like our fingers and toes.

Q. Why do some girls have more—or darker—body hair than others?

A. How much body hair you develop usually depends on your family. If your mom or dad has a lot of body hair, chances are you will too. Your ethnic background is also a factor. If your family is of Mediterranean descent, for instance, you may have more or darker body hair than someone whose family originated in the Netherlands. Also, some girls' body hair, especially arm hair, is darkest during puberty, and it becomes less prominent as they get older (though others have dark hair into adulthood).

"I hated when I started growing underarm hair. I was glad when my mom said I could shave it."

Julie, 11

Q. Why don't the women in magazines look this fuzzy?

A. In parts of Europe, they might. In some countries and cultures, body hair is considered sexy, or at least perfectly acceptable. Here in the United States, however, we tend not to like body hair very much, particularly on our legs and underarms. Eventually, you'll have to decide for yourself how you feel about it. Some girls have very fine body hair that isn't very noticeable. Some don't mind hairy legs and arms. Madonna and Julia Roberts are big celebs who've been spotted happily sporting underarm fur at one time or another. Other girls set out to annihilate every stray strand. Whatever you decide, it's best to talk to your parents about it before you do any drastic hair removal. It's not uncommon that a young girl is ready to shave her legs before her parents are ready to let her. If that's the case for you, try sitting down and explaining to your mom or dad how you feel about your body hair and why you want to remove it. Then listen to their side. See if you can reach a compromise that makes you all feel better.

Too Much Fuzz?

Body hair is a completely normal part of puberty. But lots of hair on your face or chest, especially if it seems to come overnight, can be a sign of a more serious medical condition. In that case, it's a good idea to check with your doctor to make sure everything's okay.

See also Shaving & Hair Removal, page 219.

Body Hair

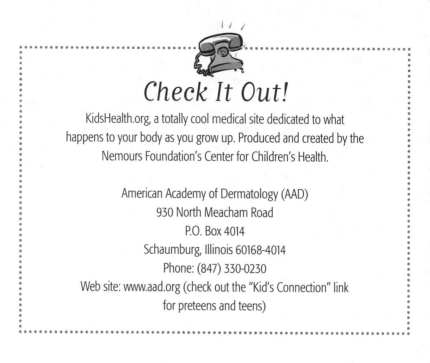

Check It Out!

KidsHealth.org, a totally cool medical site dedicated to what happens to your body as you grow up. Produced and created by the Nemours Foundation's Center for Children's Health.

American Academy of Dermatology (AAD)
930 North Meacham Road
P.O. Box 4014
Schaumburg, Illinois 60168-4014
Phone: (847) 330-0230
Web site: www.aad.org (check out the "Kid's Connection" link
for preteens and teens)

Body Hair

B.O.

The Truth About Body Odor

If you have little brothers or sisters running around, you probably notice that they don't sweat much . . . and that they don't stink much either (unless, of course, they're still in diapers—but that's another story!). During puberty, however, your sweat situation changes. The same hormones that help you grow into a woman now cause you to smell and perspire more like an adult. Though you may not be crazy about this sweaty new side of you, it's a healthy, natural thing. Sweating helps your body cool efficiently so you can play sports and have fun in the sun safely. With the right steps, sweating doesn't have to mean smelling bad. Here's what you need to know.

Q. Why does sweat stink?

A. Sweat itself actually doesn't stink at all. Problem is, many of your prominent sweat glands are under your arms, on your feet, between your legs, you get the idea—all areas on your body that don't get to "breathe" much. When you sweat in these places, moisture gets trapped, instead of evaporating away like it does from, say, your calves or your face. And the trapped moisture mixes with bacteria that all of us have on our skin. It's the bacteria that causes the odor. Then when the sweat/bacteria mixture meets the air, you notice the smell.

23

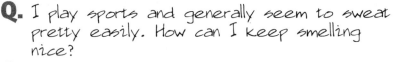

Q. I play sports and generally seem to sweat pretty easily. How can I keep smelling nice?

A. A lot of ways. Try these steps to keep smelling fresh no matter how much you sweat:

- **Hit the showers!** The less bacteria you have on your body, the less that lurks in your armpits waiting for sweat to feed on. Cut down on bacteria by showering or bathing regularly. Scrubbing every day, especially soaping up your underarms and vulva (see page 78), really helps control odor.

- **Wash those shorts.** Odor-causing bacteria can cling to your clothes, causing your shirts, shorts, socks, underpants, and whatever else to smell for days after you wear them. Keep your clothes, especially workout clothes and sports uniforms, clean.

- **Wear "wicking" fabrics.** The better your clothes breathe, the less the amount of sweat and bacteria get trapped on your body and raise a stink. When you exercise, try wearing light fabrics that are designed to pull moisture away from your body (like CoolMax or Dri-Fit). Also, if you tend to sweat even when you're not exercising, wearing natural fibers like cotton will allow your body to breathe better than other synthetic fabrics. For example, cotton underwear is a better choice than nylon for keeping your vulva region (see page 78) drier and more odor free.

- **Rub on some antiodor protection.** Puberty is the time many people start using deodorants or antiperspirants. These products, which you spray or rub under your arms—often *the* stinkiest spot of all—are very effective in fighting body odor. Deodorants cover up the odor to keep you smelling nice, and some brands fight the bacteria that cause odor, but deodorants don't actually reduce the amount of sweat you produce. Antiperspirants, on the other hand, contain chemicals that help keep you drier by reducing the amount of sweat you release. Many products are a combination of deodorant and antiperspirant. There are shelves and shelves of them at your local drugstore. Many claim to be specially made for men, women, or teens; but there's not much difference between these products besides their packaging and what they smell like (men's deodorants don't usually smell "powder fresh").

Q. I have hair under my arms. Will that make them smell worse?

A. It could. Obviously, hair doesn't stink on its own. But, like clothes, hair traps moisture and provides a breeding ground for bacteria under your arms, which, you know by now, is an area that can *definitely* contribute to body odor when you sweat. Whether to shave your underarms is a personal decision, and, of course, if you decide you want to remove the hair, your next step, before you actually do the deed, is to ask your mom. If she agrees you are old enough, she can offer advice on shaving safely. If you decide not to remove your underarm hair, just keep clean and wear deodorant. Millions of men don't shave their underarms, and they don't all stink!

Q. Why do my underarms sting when I put on deodorant?

A. Sounds like you have sensitive skin, which is pretty common. Many deodorants and antiperspirants contain strong chemicals that can irritate your skin. If that's a problem for you, try using a product for sensitive skin. Since heavy perfumes can be hard on delicate skin, you may also try using an unscented product. Also, no matter what kind of deodorant you use, it's common to experience some stinging if you apply them immediately after shaving your underarms. Remember that this is delicate skin—when you shave, don't use too much pressure and be careful not to use dull blades. And give your underarms a few minutes to recover after showering and shaving before you apply any products.

Q. How can I keep deodorant from streaking on my clothes when I get dressed?

A. When "stick" deodorants first came out, stubborn white streaks on shirts and dresses were a huge problem. Now, however, there's a big variety of clear-gel stick deodorants to choose from. These transparent products go on easily, dry quickly, and don't make a mess of your red V-neck when you pull it over your head. Another tip: When possible, apply your deodorant after you get dressed. By sneaking your deodorant on under your shirt, you avoid any risk of smudges or smears.

"School doesn't really teach you anything about the changes that girls' bodies go through. The only thing that my school did was at the end of fifth grade, teachers showed us a video and gave us some pads and deodorant."

Liz, 13

Q. One of my friends has bad B.O. Should I tell her?

A. Tough question! When you've got a friend who has a noticeable problem like bad breath or serious B.O., you have to use the Golden Rule: Do unto others as you would like them to do to you. So think of it this way: If you were walking the halls making people go "Phew!" wouldn't you want to know about it? Of course you would. The trick is telling her discreetly and nicely so she doesn't feel bad. Maybe you can try talking to her about it sometime when you're alone. Bring up that you've started wearing deodorant because you read that the hormone changes during puberty can cause body odor. If she seems interested and says that she's going to try that herself, your dilemma is solved. If she doesn't seem interested, you may have to be a little more direct and gently tell her that you've noticed that sometimes she has a little body odor, and you thought she'd want to know. She may be a little embarrassed at first, but she'll definitely be grateful you were a good friend and told her!

Q. Can I use deodorant between my legs?

A. Bad idea, though you're certainly not the first girl to think of it. Your vulva and vagina (see page 78) are some seriously sensitive spots—*not* made for the harsh chemicals in deodorants and antiperspirants. Ditto on those special "feminine hygiene" sprays and scented tampons and deodorants you may have seen in the drug store. Fragrance chemicals of any kind can cause stinging and irritation between your legs. Keep your vulva odor-free by washing daily and putting on clean cotton underpants every morning. During your period, you may want to take special precautions to stay smelling fresh. If you use a pad, the blood on your pad can become smelly if you wear it too long. Be sure to change your pad every three or four hours, even if you don't bleed heavily.

What's That Smell?

Generally speaking, your vulva area (see page 78) should be pretty odor free. It's natural that it might give off a slight odor after you've been exercising, but it shouldn't smell after a shower. If you notice that your vulva is giving off an unpleasant odor, you should mention it to your mom and see a doctor because that's a sign that you likely have a vaginal infection. Don't try to mask this smell with any kind of perfume or spray. Your doctor can prescribe the medicine you need to clear it up.

Check It Out!

American Academy of Dermatology (AAD)
930 North Meacham Road
P.O. Box 4014
Schaumburg, Illinois 60168-4014
Phone: (847) 330-0230
Web site: www.aad.org (they even have a cool link called "Kid's Connection"
for preteens and adolescents)

Eyes

Keep Those Baby Blues (or Greens, or Browns) Clear and Healthy

Someone once called the eyes "the windows to the soul." That's sweet and all, but if you can't see out of them, you'll never know whether the person looking in is someone you want to be swapping soulful gazes with. But less-than-20/20 vision can cause trouble in other places besides the romance department. For example, in the classroom; on the sports field; and, once you get that license, behind the wheel. Here are the answers you need to keep your eyes bright and your vision clear.

Q. What does 20/20 mean anyway?

A. Scientists have figured out how much a person should be able to see at a range of twenty feet—about the distance across a room in your house. When you have 20/20 vision, that means you can see everything you should be able to see at that distance. If you have 20/80 vision, that means you have to be as close as twenty feet to see what someone with normal vision can see at 80 feet.

Q. My parents both wear glasses. Does that mean I will too?

A. Depends. If your parents both needed glasses when they were your age, chances are you might need them yourself. But if your parents only started wearing glasses as adults, your vision may stay clear for a long time. Eventually, as we get older, everyone loses their perfect vision and needs the help of glasses at least now and then.

"I wear contact lenses. I'm pretty happy with them.
They are sometimes annoying to put in.
But in general, I like them."

Liz, 13

Q. How do I know if I need glasses?

A. The only way to really know is to go to an optometrist or to an eye doctor called an ophthalmologist and get your vision checked. It doesn't hurt at all—in fact, it's kind of fun to try to read the letters on the chart as the doctor makes them smaller and smaller. If books, the blackboard, or your computer screen is fuzzy or you get a lot of headaches, it's worth asking your mom or dad to take you to get a check up. The Vision Council of America says that about 25 percent of kids your age need glasses—that's one out of every four kids in your school. So you're not alone if you're having trouble seeing!

Q. What's the difference between being nearsighted and being farsighted?

A. Nearsightedness, also called myopia, means that you can see objects that are near to you, like words in a magazine, but not that are far away, like images on a movie screen or words on a chalkboard. Farsightedness means you can clearly see items far away from you, but have to work harder to see things close to you. Another common vision problem is astigmatism. That's when the front surface of your eye is shaped a little funny (something only a doctor can see), so your vision is blurred both near and far.

Q. Once I need glasses, will my vision keep getting worse the rest of my life?

A. It sure seems that way, but don't stress, your vision will settle down. Although your eyes continue to change as you continue to grow, the biggest jumps happen during puberty. Some people have a few more changes in their 20s and 30s, but your vision correction prescription should settle down about the same time as your pants size. And wearing glasses or contacts does not make your eyes worse.

Q. Is it really bad to read in the dark?

A. Reading in dim light won't hurt your eyes in any permanent way. But it does make them work harder to focus, which can strain them. If you feel like your eyes are tired or sore, or you have a headache right behind or above your eyes, it's probably a good idea to turn on some lights!

Q. Will spending too much time on the computer hurt my eyes?

A. Staring at the screen for hours as you research homework, instant-message with pals, and write papers definitely can strain your eyes or make them red and irritated. When you spend a lot of time at the computer, you tend not to blink as often as you should, so your eyes can get dry and tired. Try taking your eyes off the screen every 10 minutes or so and looking around the room or out the window. It'll give your eyes a chance to refresh.

Q. Is it okay to use drops when my eyes get red?

A. Only if you need a quick fix before a picture or class presentation. Surprisingly, those get-the-red-out drops can actually

Eyes

leave your eyes more bloodshot. They work by shrinking the blood vessels that are creeping across the whites of your eyes. But it's just a temporary solution. When the drops wear off, those vessels swell up even larger. Better to try drops that help your eyes heal themselves, like artificial tears.

"I got my eyes checked by a doctor
to be sure that I could see. It was kind of fun,
and I didn't need glasses, which is good."

Kortni, 10

Q. How can I keep my eyes healthy? Is eating carrots really good for them?

A. Carrots are great. But sunglasses rule. You can't see or feel it happening, but every time you go out in the sun without your shades, you're doing a little damage to your eyes. Over your lifetime, that adds up and can contribute to sight-threatening eye diseases. Sunglasses look cool, so they're fun to wear anyway. Check the tag for the words "Meets ANSI Standards for UVA and UVB Rays" when you're buying sunglasses so you know you're getting full protection. In bright sun, it's also a good idea to wear a wide-brimmed hat or a baseball cap.

You already know that smoking stinks up your hair and causes wrinkles, well, it also causes damage to your eyes that over time can lead to cataracts. So passing on the butts is another good way to protect your eyes.

If you wear makeup, avoid sharing eye shadow, mascara, and other stuff that goes around your eyes. If you do share shadow, use throw away sponges or Q-tips to put it on. Use makeup remover to take it off at night. Don't spit on tissues to remove smeary mascara or eyeliner—your mouth has lots of germs you don't want in your eyes!

As far as the carrots go, munch away. And while you're at it, add some other brightly colored fruits and vegetables, like

Eyes

cantaloupe, broccoli, leafy greens, and oranges. These foods contain chemicals that fight the damage done by sunlight and pollution.

Q. When can I start to wear contacts?

A. When you're ready for the responsibility of caring for lenses. That's the only real criteria the doctors have. Contact lenses have gotten a whole lot easier to wear and care for since the days of hard lenses that popped out of your eyes at the worst times. But they still need to be kept clean. Dirty, poorly handled lenses can lead to scratched eyes, infections, and, worse, an ulcer in your eye—bad news! If you get contacts, always follow your doctor's instructions carefully.

Q. How old do I have to be to get laser surgery to fix my eyes?

A. You have to be 18 to have corrective vision surgery. And even then, it's probably a good idea to wait a few more years, as doctors keep track of the long-term effects of the surgery.

Keep an Eye on Your Eyesight!

Any time you have a change in vision or pain in your eyes, you should see an optometrist. If you wear contact lenses, you need to be especially alert. If you have blurred or fuzzy vision (especially if it comes on suddenly), red, irritated eyes, discomfort wearing your lenses, or pain in or around your eyes, see your doctor.

Check It Out!

American Academy of Ophthalmology
P.O. Box 7424
San Francisco, California 94120
Phone: (415) 561-8500
Web site: www.aao.org

American Optometric Association
243 North Lindbergh Boulevard
St. Louis, Missouri 63141
Phone: (314) 991-4100
Fax: (314) 991-4101
Web site: www.aoanet.org

Feet

One Step Ahead of You

Though they look pretty simple, your feet are surprisingly complex—and way important. Each foot has 26 bones and 33 joints, and small, big, or in between, your feet are the only thing supporting your entire body as you walk, jump, and run—which is a lot. The average kid takes more than 18,000 steps a day! Like your breasts and hips, your feet are probably sprouting as we speak. Since nothing can stop you in your tracks like aching tootsies, it's important to take care of your growing feet the best you can. Here are the steps you need to know.

Q. My feet are almost the size of my mom's already! I'm afraid they're going to be gigantic. What gives?

A. Take a load off your mind—and your feet! Your feet are often the first thing to grow as you start puberty. Think about it. Your body is ready to start its biggest growth spurt yet. You wouldn't want to be teetering around on tiny baby feet, would you? Of course not. That's why your body's smart enough to make your feet grow first, so they're strong enough to support the rest of you as your body catches up.

Q. Can I tell how big my feet will be?

A. Nope. Just as you can't be 100 percent sure how tall you'll end up, you can't predict your shoe size. They may be similar to the size of your mom's feet, but it's not unusual for them to be bigger. In fact, the average foot size has increased steadily over the past fifty years, so the average woman now wears a size nine instead of a size eight. Your feet will pretty much be done growing by the time you're between 15 and 17. Though they may get a little bigger later on in adulthood, the majority of the growth happens early in puberty.

Q. How do I know if my shoes fit right?

A. Good question! Many adults don't even know the answer to that question, and they walk around in shoes that are too tight or too loose. Some experts estimate that around 70 percent of foot problems come from wearing the wrong footwear or poorly fitting shoes. So finding comfortable, properly fitting shoes is one of the most important things you can do for the health and happiness of your feet. When buying new shoes, try to shop at the end of the day when your feet are at their biggest (your feet swell during the day). The ball of your foot—that's the wide part beneath your toes—should fit comfortably in the widest part of the shoe. The heel should be snug and not slip up and down when you walk. And your toes should not be smooshed against the front of the shoe. There should be about a half-inch (about the width of your thumb) of room from the tip of your longest toe to the tip of the shoe. Because your feet are growing so fast right now, it's a good idea to always have them measured before you buy a new pair.

Q. Are high heels really so bad for you?

A. Wearing high heels occasionally, like for a special event or dance, is not going to hurt your feet. But wearing high heels— any shoe with heels more than one inch high—every day or several times a week can affect the growth of your feet and can cause foot problems. High heels are not good for your knees or the connective tissue in your ankles either.

Q. My doctor says my feet are flat. What does that mean? And is it bad?

A. Having flat feet means that you have very little arch in your foot. If you look at the inside edge of people's feet, you'll notice that most people's feet sweep up into an arch from the ball of their foot to their heel. If you have flat feet, you have very little sweep, maybe none at all. Flat feet are very, very common, and it's not "bad" to have them, though they sometimes do cause problems. When your feet are flat, they don't absorb shock as well as they would if you had arches. So when you run around, you end up taking more shock in other parts of your body, like your knees and hips. Some people with flat feet get pain in their shins or their knees when they run. People with flat feet also may have more foot problems down the road. But you may live happily forever with your flat feet and never have a problem. The best thing to do is see a special doctor called a podiatrist about your flat feet. He or she can measure your feet and watch the way you walk to see if your flat feet are something to be concerned about. If they are, it's pretty easy to keep flat feet from being a pain simply by putting special inserts called *orthotics* into your shoes.

"I already wear a size nine—the same size as my mom! I hope my feet stop growing soon."

Julie, 11

Q. Why do my feet stink?

A. Because they sweat! Here's a gross but true foot fact: There are more sweat glands per square inch on your feet (about 250,000 total) than anywhere else on your body. The average pair of feet

Feet

can sweat out about half a pint—that's two cups!—of perspiration a day. But they don't have to smell bad just because they sweat. The best way to prevent foot odor is to wear socks because they absorb the sweat, and always try to wear shoes made from leather or fabrics like canvas, nylon, and mesh because they let your feet breathe—then all that moisture doesn't get trapped in your shoes and start to reek. Shoes made out of plastic, rubber, or fake leather can turn your feet into sweatboxes—and maybe stinkboxes. Here's a tip: Sprinkling a little baking soda in your shoes can help absorb any unpleasant odor. Just be sure to shake out the powder before you wear them to keep from getting dusty white feet.

Q. What causes blisters?

A. You get blisters from wearing shoes that don't fit right and rub against spots on your feet. After enough rubbing, the skin layers in that spot begin to separate (ouch!) and fill with fluid, forming a painful bubble. It's really tempting to pop blisters, but they can get infected that way, so you shouldn't. Just put a Band-Aid over the area to protect it and let it heal. And always buy shoes that fit just right.

Q. Why do I get warts on my feet?

A. Warts and other infections—like athlete's foot, a condition that causes your feet to peel, burn, and itch—are caused by fungi and viruses that get passed from person to person, especially in public places like locker room showers and swimming pools. Athlete's foot is easy to treat with sprays and powders you can buy at the drugstore. But warts can be a little harder. Though there are some products you can buy to put on warts, it can take a long, long time for them to work—if they ever do. So it's probably easier and faster to see your doctor if you have warts on your feet.

Feet

Protect Your Toes

Don't forget to cut your toenails! It's easy to neglect them, 'til they start curling around your toes or jamming against the front of your shoes when you run. Keep an eye on your toenails and trim them regularly—about every two weeks. For the best results, cut your toenails after you shower, when they're softest, and use a toenail clipper (it's bigger and easier to use than a little nail clipper). Cut your nails straight across to avoid ingrown toenails, a painful condition when the sharp corner of a toenail grows into the skin on the side of your toe—yikes!

Check It Out!

American Podiatric Medical Association
9312 Old Georgetown Road
Bethesda, Maryland 20814
Phone: (800) ASK-APMA (275-2762), (301) 571-9200
Web site: www.apma.org

Feet

Hair

Keeping Your Locks
Looking Their Best

L et's face the facts: Our hair is a *major* part of who we are and how we look. Whether you've got a flowing mane, à la Britney Spears, or you crop it pixie close like Pink, your hair frames your facial features and helps complement your style. So it's natural to experiment with braids, bands, bandanas, curls, and more to express how you're feeling on any given day, whether you're dressing up for a dance or going totally casual for a game. The trick to great-looking hair no matter what the style is keeping it healthy. Here are the hair-care answers you need.

Q. How fast does my hair grow?

A. Hair usually grows about one-half inch a month, a little faster in the warm seasons like summer. Not all your hair grows at the same time. Every hair on your head grows for about two to six years, then it rests. So some hair is always resting while the rest is growing.

Q. There's a lot of hair in the drain after I shower. Am I losing my hair?

A. Yep! But no need to panic, we all lose hair all the time. What you see in the shower drain, and in your hair brush, is part of the fifty to a hundred hairs we normally shed every day. Even though that sounds like a lot, you don't miss those hairs, because new ones grow to take their place. The average head of hair has about 100,000 hairs on it, so there are plenty of strands up there at all times.

"I like to experiment with different haircuts.
I like to always look different!"

Tara, 13

Q. I hear about lice in my school and it grosses me out. How can I avoid it?

A. It's natural to feel creepy about the thought of bugs living anywhere on you, let alone in your hair. But try not to get too freaked. Head lice are pretty common in schools, so it's not impossible that you or someone you know could catch them. Chances are you won't, though, since it's not like every school kid gets them. The important thing is if you or someone you know gets lice, it's not because you're dirty or that anything's wrong with you. You were just in the wrong place at the wrong time. Lice are basically small gray parasites that live in human hair. They bite your scalp, which leaves an itchy sore, and they lay a *ton* of tiny white eggs, so it's important to get rid of them fast! The eggs, called nits, are usually found around your hairline or above your ears. There are very good delousing products at the drug store, such as special shampoos and combs to kill and remove every last louse (the singular of lice) and nit. By the way, if you ever accuse someone of "nitpicking" that's where the phrase comes from. Since nits are so tiny, we refer to someone who picks at tiny problems as a nitpicker.

You can protect yourself from lice by taking a few precautions: Don't share anything that comes in contact with your head and hair with friends. That includes combs; brushes; hair accessories; hats; headphones; and, if you're having a sleepover, even pillows. It sounds extreme, but, especially if you know there's been lice at your school, it's just good hygiene.

Q. What causes split ends?

A. If you don't keep your hair trimmed, the ends will fray like a loose piece of fabric. Remember how your hair grows about a half inch a month? Well if your locks are over your shoulders, those last couple of inches have been through a couple of *years* of wear and tear! That's why even if you're growing your hair out, it's important to get the ends trimmed every couple of months. What if you already have frayed ends? Don't sweat it. Even if you have four inches of damaged hair, just a few appointments with a hairstylist will fix it right up. Just have a half inch taken off every month 'til all the hair that's left is split-end free. Then make a point of getting a regular trim—every other month or so. Also, go easy on the blow dryer and styling products; too much heat can contribute to split ends.

"I don't change my hair much. Maybe twice a year.
I just like being me."

Ashlyn, 13

Q. What's better, combs or brushes?

A. Depends on your hair type and style. A brush may not do much for super short cuts, and a comb doesn't always do the job for longer styles. Whatever tool you choose, make sure it's a product that won't damage your hair. Look for brushes with round-tipped bristles and use a wide-tooth comb if you're prone to tangles. Remember, if you do have knots, comb from the bottom up, working through small sections of the tangle. Don't try to just yank the comb through. Also, don't brush your hair when it's wet. Wet hair is weaker than dry hair, so brushing can actually break it. Comb it instead.

Q. How often should I wash my hair?

A. That's a controversial topic. A lot of girls like washing their hair every day, especially girls going through puberty, when their oil glands are more active and their hair can feel oily. Many hair experts caution against overwashing, however, because it strips natural oil from your hair and actually may cause your hair follicles to produce more oil to make up for the loss. For most people, daily washing is unnecessary, and you can just rinse your hair if you're showering. However, if you use a lot of hair products, like gels and sprays, or you're very active and sweat a lot, washing more often may be a good idea. Experiment to see what works best for you. If you're prone to tangly hair, you may also want to use a conditioner after you shampoo to help keep it smooth.

Q. I love playing with hair styles, but my mom says a lot of blow drying, crimping, and flat ironing will wreck my hair. Is that true?

A. As fun as they are to use, hair-care tools like dryers, curling irons, crimpers, and flat irons can literally fry your hair! Hardly the style you're going for. A few hair protection steps can help you use these tools safely:

- **Let your hair air-dry about three quarters dry.** If it's only damp instead of soaking wet before you start to blow-dry it, it'll spend less time under intense heat.

- **Add protection.** Don't use intense heat-styling tools like flat irons and curling irons without protecting your hair first. Putting a silicone-based hair protection product like Frizz-Ease on your hair before styling can help keep it from drying out.

Hair

- **Give it a break.** Crimping out like Christina Aguilera is fun for a weekend party. But do you really need a big wavy mane for Monday morning biology? Give your hair regular breaks from all the muss and fuss. That way it'll look healthy and shiny every day.

Q. I swim several times a week. How can I keep the chlorine in the pool from drying out my hair?

A. If you swim a lot, it's a good idea to use a conditioner regularly, because it provides a protective layer for your hair. Also, rinse your hair as soon as you get out of the pool. That removes a lot of the chlorine. There are a lot of great shampoos, like Ultra Swim, that can remove chlorine from your hair. If you have a lot of chlorine buildup on your hair, you may notice that your hair has a dry, thick, glassy appearance. You can buy a detoxifying shampoo like Citre Shine to remove that kind of chlorine buildup. One hair type needs special care: very light blonde. If you've got almost white-blonde hair, chlorine will turn your hair green. There are special oil sprays you can spritz on your hair before you swim that'll keep you from looking like Kermit when you get out. Ask your hairstylist to recommend one.

Q. What can I do if I get a horrible haircut?

A. *Everyone* gets a haircut they hate at least once in their life. It's definitely a big drag, but it's not the end of the world. First, give yourself a day to chill out and try styling your new cut yourself. Sometimes you may not like the way someone blows out your hair, but the cut's really okay once you wash and style it yourself. If you still hate it, make an appointment with another stylist. Sometimes it helps to ask around for recommendations. If you have friends with great hair who are happy with their stylists, that might be a good place to go yourself. Tell the stylist what you're unhappy about and listen to what he or she suggests. Chances are the new stylist will be able to make adjustments that'll make you happier with your new 'do, at least 'til it grows out. And remember, bad haircuts are totally temporary.

In just a few weeks, it'll grow out and you'll have new styling options. The best way to avoid bad cuts is to find a stylist you trust and who understands what you like and don't like in a haircut. Also, tempting as it can be, *never* cut your own hair. It's harder than it looks and almost always ends up needing a repair job.

"I don't experiment with hairstyles that much because whenever I do, it ends up looking like a disaster."

Liz, 13

Q. How do I know if I have dandruff?

A. It's hard to miss. Dandruff causes you to shed flakes of skin from your scalp that fall from your hair onto your clothes like tiny snowflakes on your shoulders. It also makes your scalp dry and itchy. In most cases, you can clear up dandruff with a dandruff shampoo like Head and Shoulders, that you can buy from a drugstore. If that doesn't work, ask your mom to take you to a dermatologist for stronger treatment.

Q. How can I get my mom to agree to let me color my hair a funky color?

A. Though it's *your* hair and it's understandable that you feel like you should be able to do what you like with it, you have to respect your mom's restrictions on big hair changes. Just like she wouldn't necessarily let you wear a shimmery tube top to school, she may not be hot on having you walking around with purple hair. Remember, too, a lot of schools also have restrictions on how wild you can wear your hair. It doesn't seem fair, but it's really just getting you ready for having a job because a lot of employers won't hire people with crazy hairstyles either. Hair projects an image, and if your image doesn't agree with theirs, you're out.

That said, there's almost always some kind of compromise. Maybe your mom will agree to some fun highlights or a cute new cut that you can make funky with hair clips, glitter sprays, and bands. There are even some temporary colors that you can spray or wash in, but that will wash out. Don't forget, your mom may just be looking out for you. Permanent hair color lasts a long time and if you get tired of the pink in a couple weeks (and hairstylists say this happens *all the time*), you're pretty much stuck with it. Finally, even if your mom agrees to a certain color change or perm, your stylist may say that it's not a good idea. Your hair is still developing in your preteen years. Until you've gone through puberty, the core of your hair isn't fully formed. That means your hair is softer and won't take as well to chemical processes like colors and perms as adult hair. So until your hair is ready, it's a good idea to stick to gentler products, like semi-permanent colors, and opt for a good versatile cut that will let you play with different styles.

Q. I play sports. What hairstyle will work best for me?

A. One that is easy to take care of and doesn't get in your way while you play. What works best for many active girls is wearing hair in one length or long layers about to their shoulders. That gives them plenty of hair to play with when they want to dress it up, but it's also a cinch to pull back into a ponytail come game time.

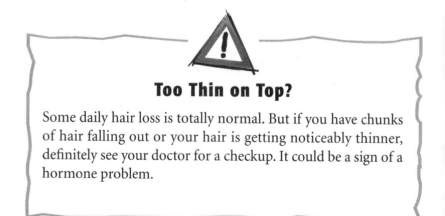

Too Thin on Top?

Some daily hair loss is totally normal. But if you have chunks of hair falling out or your hair is getting noticeably thinner, definitely see your doctor for a checkup. It could be a sign of a hormone problem.

Check It Out!

Web site: www.hair-care.com (full of tips and fun articles about having healthy, great-looking hair)

Height

Up, Up, and Away!

One of the coolest parts of growing up is just that—literally growing up. Adults who used to tower over you now look you straight in the eye, and you finally feel like one of the "big kids" when you walk down the halls at school. Right now, as you enter and go through puberty, is the biggest period of rapid growth you've had since you were a baby! Here are some answers to the most commonly asked questions about growing.

Q. Everyone's getting taller but me. When will I start to grow?

A. Depends how close you are to getting your period. Before puberty, the average girl grows about two inches per year. Once girls hit puberty that is, begin developing breasts and body hair, they shoot up like weeds, adding several inches in a single year. Once a girl gets her period, however, the growth spurt slows back down to one or two inches a year. Though every girl gets her period at a different time, for most girls the biggest growth spurt happens between their eleventh and twelfth birthdays. Most girls then add two or three more inches, reaching adult height by about their fifteenth birthday, though it's possible to grow a little more in your late teens. So be patient!

Once your growth spurt starts, you'll be adding inches just like your friends.

Q. I just started really growing. Can I tell how tall I will be?

A. There's no crystal ball or psychic hotline that can tell you what your final height will be, but there is a formula doctors use that can get you pretty close.

1. First, find out how tall your mom and dad are (since this equation is based on heredity, these numbers need to be from your birth parents; stepparents won't work).

2. Subtract five inches from your dad's height.

3. Add that number (your dad's height minus five inches) to your mom's height.

4. Divide that number by two.

5. That's your estimated height!

For instance, let's say your dad is six feet tall and your mom is five feet, six inches tall. When you subtract five inches from six feet you get five feet, seven inches (remember there are twelve inches in a foot). When you add five feet, seven inches to five feet, six inches you get eleven feet, one inch. And finally, divide that by two—you can expect to be about five feet, five and a half inches.

Q. I'm super short, and I hate it. Is there anything I can do to make myself taller?

A. Sorry, but no. You can't stretch yourself or eat tons of spinach and hope to add inches to your frame. Your height is not something you can change. But you don't have to hate it. What probably gets you down is how *other* people react to your height. They may make jokes or call you names, like, say, "shrimp." Adults may mistake you for being younger than you are—*definitely* annoying. People also tend to think of small things as "cute," so you may feel like you're not being taken as

Height

seriously as you'd like. The solution is to hold your head high and act the same way you want to be treated. Ignore the jokes (people usually stop making them if they don't get a reaction), speak up when you have something to say, and be yourself. Soon people will see you for your personality and ideas, not your height.

Q. I'm only thirteen, and I'm already five feet, eight inches! I hate being so tall. What can I do?

A. Just like you can't make yourself taller, you can't make yourself shrink either. Though it can be tough towering over everyone at a time in your life when you often want to just blend in, many women today love being tall. A lot of the women you probably admire in sports, in magazines, and on television are tall. In fact, there are few models who don't stand at least five feet, seven inches. So take heart. You may not be the happiest about your height now, but chances are your feelings will change. In the meantime, don't try to hide your height by slumping or slouching—that just makes you look like a tall girl with bad posture. Stand proud and be happy for who you are. Remember, there are plenty of girls who would love to have your height.

"I'm small and I don't like it. I haven't noticed signs of puberty like getting taller or needing a bra yet. Sometimes I feel a little weird."

Samantha, 9

Q. Why are all the boys in my class so much shorter than the girls?

A. They haven't hit their growth spurt yet. But don't worry, that'll change. Girls just get a head start—on average, boys end up

Height

taller than girls. While you and your girlfriends started sprouting skyward around age eleven or twelve, most boys go through their growth spurt later in puberty, around age thirteen or fourteen. After that, you might find yourself looking upward at all those boys who seem so short today.

---

*"I'm average to tall for my age.
I am very happy with my height."*

Britany, 11

Q. Does drinking coffee really stunt your growth?

A. Probably not, though it's not a good idea to drink gallons of the stuff—or of anything else that contains a lot of caffeine, like colas and other soft drinks. Caffeine steals calcium from your bones, which may not end up making you shorter, but could end up leaving your bones weaker. It's better to stick to bone-building beverages like milk, as well as juice and water, which don't necessarily build bone (although many juices these days have calcium added), but won't hurt them either.

Another thing that people say can stunt your growth is smoking. Again, smoking probably won't make you shorter, but there are *lots* of other reasons you should steer clear of cigarettes. Smoking definitely hurts your bones. In fact, if you look at pictures of the bones of women who have been smoking for years, they look like Swiss cheese, filled with giant holes. That's the last thing you need happening at a time when you're building bones that will have to last you your whole life!

Avoid the "Growth Stunters"

Now more than ever you need to eat well and get plenty of exercise. Because you're growing at a rapid pace—up to four inches a year!—your bones need plenty of calcium and other nutrients to stay strong. Avoid dieting, a lot of junk food, and definitely smoking. All these things can rob your bones of important vitamins and minerals they need to grow.

Check It Out!

American Academy of Pediatrics
141 Northwest Point Boulevard
Elk Grove Village, Illinois 60007-1098
Phone: (847) 434-4000
Web site: www.aap.org

Height

Hips

Shake Your Booty

Curves: They're what make you different from the boy next door. As you move through puberty, your breasts give you new curves up top and your widening hips produce booty-shaking curves below your waist. Some girls greet these developments with a resounding "Hip, hip, hooray!" while others are less than thrilled with their ever-changing physique. However you feel right now, chances are you'll learn to like your new body as you grow into it. Here's the deal on those new hippy curves and how to care for them.

Q. Why do my hips get wide when boys' hips don't?

A. Two words: Estrogen and babies. During puberty, your ovaries start producing more *estrogen*—the hormone that helps turn you from a girl to a young woman. One of the things estrogen does is encourage healthy body fat on your hips (since your hip bones are also increasing in size, this extra weight is normal and necessary). Down the road you'll find that having wider hips than guys makes it easier for you to deliver a baby. Plus life would be totally boring if boys and girls looked the same!

Q. Is my butt part of my hips? Does my butt change, too?

A. Your butt is actually a muscle—the *gluteus maximus*—so it's not technically part of your hips, which are the pelvic bones and the flesh around them. However, both your butt and hips are definitely in the same region. As for whether your butt changes, let's face it—there's very little about you that *doesn't* change during puberty, your butt included. But don't bug out because your booty is filling out. Your muscles (remember, your butt's a muscle) need to get bigger and stronger as you grow up. And the padding around your breasts, butt, and hips makes your waist look smaller, giving you more womanly curves.

"I used to have no hips at all. Now I'm starting to need new jeans. At first I didn't like it. But now I think I like having some curves."

Julie, 11

Q. Will having wider hips change the way I play sports?

A. Maybe, maybe not. For some girls, their widening hips change the way their legs are shaped, bringing their knees closer together and adding a little flair outward below the knees. This can increase your risk for knee injuries (see Knees, page 57). Fortunately, learning proper technique, wearing the right shoes, and keeping your legs strong can reduce your risk for these problems. If you participate in sports like gymnastics and skating, where you're flipping your body in space, your changing body may throw you off now and then; but that's nothing you can't adjust to.

Hips

Q. Why can my best friend do the splits, but I can't even get close to the floor? Are her hips different from mine?

A. The only difference is that her hips are more flexible than yours. Girls' hormones make their joints naturally more supple, and some girls seem almost "double-jointed," or so flexible that they can do things like splits without blinking an eye. Girls who are superlimber tend to be good at sports like gymnastics and cheerleading, but they also have to be careful about not dislocating their joints. The best way to do that: Keep the muscles that support those joints strong. Ask your coach or gym teacher for the best exercises.

Beware of Stiff or "Clicking" Hips

In most cases your hips grow without much ado. But sometimes the growing end, or the "growth plate," of your *femur* (the thigh bone) slips off the top of the thigh bone, creating a condition called *slipped capital femoral epiphysis* (SCFE). This can happen on its own during a growth spurt or during a trauma like a sports injury or fall. It's more common in boys, but it happens in girls, too. If you have SCFE, your hips may feel stiff or painful. You may also feel pain in your knee or groin or a click in your hip. You may also have trouble moving your hips or even start limping. If you have any of these symptoms, have your doctor check them out. If you catch SCFE early, a pretty simple surgery can make you good as new.

Hips

Check It Out!

American Academy of Orthopaedic Surgeons
6300 North River Road
Rosemont, Illinois 60018-4262
Phone: (800) 346-AAOS (2267)
Web site: www.aaos.org

Knees
Your Most Helpful Hinges

You probably don't spend much time thinking about your knees. But the joints between your upper and lower legs let you do some of the best stuff in life—dance, run, ride a bike, participate in sports like soccer—that's why it's super important to treat your knees right. Growing girls are more susceptible to certain knee injuries than boys are, and an injury can keep you on the sidelines when you'd rather be playing. Here's what you need to know about knee care.

Q. I've heard that sports like basketball and soccer are risky for my knees. But I love these sports. What can I do to protect my knees?

A. Don't give up your favorite sports! It's true, girls who play sports that involve a lot of quick jumping, turning, and landing—like basketball, soccer, and volleyball—are more prone to dislocating their kneecaps, tearing their meniscus (the cartilage cushion inside the knee), or injuring knee ligaments like the *anterior cruciate ligament* (the band commonly called the ACL that runs behind your kneecap and connects your thigh bone to your shin bone). That's because as girls' hips widen during puberty, the angle where the thigh bone connects to the knee changes and puts more stress on the knees. In fact, girls are four to six times more likely to get an ACL injury than boys of the same age.

So what's an active gal to do? First, you need to learn to jump, land, and twist correctly. Ask your coach to go through drills teaching you the proper way to perform these movements. The coach will probably be happy to teach the whole team because it means fewer injuries for everybody. Next, make sure your leg muscles are good and strong, to support your knees. Sometimes what happens is that a girl grows so fast, her thigh muscles don't develop in time to protect her knees while she's playing sports. Again, ask your coach to recommend a few exercises to keep your *hamstrings* (the muscles on the backs of your upper legs) and your *quadriceps* (the muscles on the front of your upper legs) strong. Some researchers say by doing just those two things—using proper technique and having strong thigh muscles—you can cut your risk of knee injury by more than two-thirds! Other ways to protect yourself: Wear the right shoes! If you play hoops, wear basketball shoes. If soccer's your thing, wear the right cleats. Proper footwear helps keep you on your feet and injury-free. Also, try to stay active year-round. If you're a sofa slug nine months out of the year, then you dash out to be a soccer babe for three months in the fall, you're more likely to hurt yourself than if your knees are used to running, jumping, and playing 365 days a year!

Q. What causes knock-knees?

A. It's all about angles. In girls, especially as they hit puberty and their hips get wider, the thigh bones angle inward to the knees. That's true for all girls. However, in some girls this angle is really exaggerated, creating that knock-kneed look. Knock-knees won't hurt you and are fairly common. Most kids grow out of knock-knees by the time they're eight years old. If you are very knock-kneed and it bothers you, talk to your parents about seeing a special kind of doctor called an orthopedist (a "bone doctor"), preferably one who specializes in sports medicine. He or she may be able to help make you more comfortable.

Q. My knees hurt when I run. Is that normal?

A. Pain is never normal. Whenever your body hurts, it's trying to tell you something's up. In this case, it's probably saying, "Hey! My kneecaps are slipping around a little and it's not comfortable!" Like other knee woes, kneecaps that slide out of place some are pretty common in active girls. Again, strong thigh muscles, good shoes, and good running form are the best ways to protect yourself. Ask your coach to give you exercises to help get those legs strong and to look at your running form, too, just to make sure you're doing everything A-okay. If you're not in sports, talk to your phys-ed teacher or a sports medicine doctor. And remember that your body needs time to adjust to any sport or activity. So if you're not used to running and suddenly go out and try to run two miles, it's likely that something will hurt. Start easy and increase the time and distance you run by a little bit each week.

Q. Will wearing knee braces help keep my knees safe?

A. Maybe. But they can also do more harm than good. Think of it this way: A knee brace supports your knee, so it is less likely to go out of whack. But if you rely on it too much, the muscles you need to support that hinge of yours will get lazy and provide even less protection when you aren't wearing the brace. Get a doctor's okay before using any kind of brace to play.

Q. Why is the skin on my knees so rough and scaly?

A. It's common for the skin over joints like your elbows and knees to get a little rough and dry, especially if you're active and spend a lot of time outdoors. A simple way to keep that skin smooth is to use a soapy mesh scrubby or a body sponge and gently rub those areas while you're in the shower. Then apply lotion to them, and to any other dry areas, as soon as you're out of the shower. You can reapply lotion more often if your skin tends to be dry.

Take Injuries Seriously!

Though nobody likes to sit out while others are on the field, playing on a bum knee will only make it worse, and could keep you out of the game much, much longer. As soon as you feel pain, stop what you're doing and let your coach and mom or dad know what happened. In many cases, you'll just need to rest it and ice it for a few days. Sometimes you may need additional treatment. In any case, it's important to let your body heal before you run back out and start playing again.

Check It Out!

American Academy of Orthopaedic Surgeons
6300 North River Road
Rosemont, Illinois 60018-4262
Phone: (800) 346-AAOS (2267)
Web site: www.aaos.org

Nails

The Unpolished Facts

Many girls regard fingernails as nothing more than a place to put fun-colored polish. But if you've ever had to scratch your back or if you've ever closed your fingers in a door (ouch!), you know that the hard shells on top of your fingertips are more than just decoration. They serve a useful purpose, protecting your fingers and providing a convenient "tool" for scratching itches and picking up tiny items. Similarly, your toenails give your piggies a little extra protection when they're bumped or stepped on. Like the rest of you, your nails change as you grow up, becoming a little thicker and stronger. Here's how to keep them healthy and looking their best.

Q. I want to grow my nails. How long will it take?

A. How patient are you? Fingernails grow at the snail's pace of 0.1 mm a day, which ends up being less than one inch a year. Of course, when one breaks, you have to start over again. While it may be fun to try growing your nails, it's really not worth the time and hassle if you're an active girl. A better look: Keep them short with squared off tips. This is the style even most celebrities—who need to keep their hands looking good—wear today. Nails this length look great and they're less prone to breaking.

> "I mostly like painting my nails blue.
> But white is great because it matches everything."

Tara, 13

Q. Should I use a nail clipper or a nail file?

A. Both! About once a week, trim the tips of your nails with a nail clipper. Then, with a file or emery board (a popsicle stick–shaped board with a sandpapery surface), round off the corners on either side of your nails and smooth out any rough edges. And don't forget your toenails. Left too long, they can start curling around your toes and poking into the skin. Toenails grow a little slower than fingernails, so you only have to cut them about every two weeks. Use a larger toenail clipper (if your parents have one, otherwise a fingernail clipper will do) and trim your toenails straight across.

> "My favorite color used to be red, but then I
> found out that it turns your nails yellow.
> Now my favorite color is pink."

Liz, 13

Q. Does wearing nail polish hurt your nails?

A. Nope. Polish, decals, rhinestones, and glitter won't hurt your fingernails—or toenails—though some makeup artists find that wearing a lot of polish all the time can make your nails a little dry. You'll also notice that if you wear nail polish all the time, your nails can end up turning a yellowish color, because they get stained from the polish. So even if you love polish, it might be a good idea to let your nails go bare every once in a while, give them a breather for a couple days.

Q. How can I stop biting my nails?

A. Good question! Because biting your nails does more than make your nails look bad. One of the biggest ways that you pick up germs and viruses that make you sick is by putting your fingers in your mouth. So nail biting is definitely a good habit to break! But how?! One way is by making your nails taste bad. You can buy special nail polish at the drug store that tastes sour or bitter, then every time your fingers get near your mouth you get a rude reminder not to bite your nails. Another way is to keep your fingers busy. Sometimes we bite or pick at our nails just because we're bored. Carry around a string of beads or one of those smooth worry stones that you can use to keep your fingers busy and away from your teeth. Finally, set goals. Tell yourself that if you don't bite your nails for a week, you'll do something special for yourself.

"I like painting my nails baby blue.
That color looks nice with everything."

Kortni, 10

Q. I play outside a lot, and my nails get really dirty. How should I clean them?

A. Dirt and grime under your fingernails comes with outdoor fun. But it certainly doesn't look good in the classroom or at the dinner table. First, wash your hands with warm soapy water. That helps soften up the dirt and wash the worst of it away. Then you can use the nail cleaner that's attached to your nail clippers. It's a long pointed file that swings out from inside the clippers (be careful, it can be a little sharp). Use the curved pointy end to scrape out the remaining dirt from under your nails. Or, if your parents have one, you can use a special nailbrush to scrub away the grime.

Q. What can I do to make my nails stronger?

A. For years people thought eating Jell-O would make your nails strong. But that was never proven. The best way to ensure healthy, strong nails is to take good care of the rest of your body. Eat a balanced diet filled with fruits, vegetables, whole grains, milk and other dairy foods, and healthy protein foods like beans, fish, poultry, and lean meats. Drink plenty of water. And get eight or nine hours of sleep every night. That's the recipe for healthy skin, hair, and nails.

Nails

Mend Those Splits!

Most of the time, caring for nails is a no-brainer. But occasionally you can end up with a painful condition called a *hangnail*. This isn't actually a nail at all, but a nasty split in the skin alongside your nail. It hurts as it dangles there and catches on things, but resist the urge to bite or pick at it. You'll only aggravate it and make it hurt worse. Instead, take a nail clipper and trim the hangnail as close to the bottom of it as possible. If it's red and sore, clean it with soap and water, put a Band-Aid on it, and leave it alone for a couple of days. It should heal quickly.

Check It Out!

Web site: www.e-fingernail.com (more facts about fingernails than you ever thought you'd want to know!)

Skin

The "Clothes" Your Growing Body Lives In

Wanna hear something cool? By the time you're done growing, you'll have eighteen to twenty square feet of skin on your body—enough to carpet a small room! Your skin weighs more than five pounds. And the outside layer sheds constantly. In fact, enough dead skin cells rub off and enough new cells form to give you a whole new skin every month—that's almost a thousand new skins in your lifetime. It's a little gross when you think about it, but by the time you're seventy years old, you'll have shed more than a hundred pounds of skin. Look around at the dust in your house—some of that is really dead skin cells that have fallen off your body!

Though it doesn't look like your heart or a kidney, your skin is actually an organ. It grows and changes with you. It's your main source of protection from the environment, and let's not forget it's the first thing everyone sees, so it's *way* important to take care of it. Here's the skinny on your skin.

 Q. Is the sun really so bad for me?

A. Actually, you need sunlight to live! When your skin is exposed to sunshine, it actually *makes* vitamin D—a nutrient you need to develop strong bones. Though you can also get vitamin D from fortified milk, it's important not to shun the sun. That said, you don't need to strap on a bikini and fry like a chicken to make vitamin D. Ten minutes of sun on your hands and face is all you need. Excessive exposure not only leads to sunburns, but, over time, also ages your skin by causing spots and wrinkles. And it causes skin cancer—about one million cases every year. That's why it's important to use sunscreen with a sun protection factor (SPF) of at least 15 whenever you're going to be outside for more than a few minutes. Follow the directions on the label for when and how often to apply it. (See Sunshine, page 237, for more sun protection tips.)

Of course, it's fun to play in the sun, and life would be lame if all you did was sit inside all day. It's just important to protect yourself with sunscreen. When chilling outdoors, look for a sunscreen that offers "broad spectrum" protection—that means it protects against both UVA and UVB ultraviolet radiation. It should have an SPF rating of at least 15. If you're going to be kicking it on the beach all day, especially between 10:00 A.M.and 4:00 P.M. when the sun is at its strongest, you should use a sun-*block* that contains titanium dioxide or zinc oxide. Don't forget around your eyes, your ears, and your lips. And remember, the sun's rays penetrate your skin even on cloudy days, so it's a good idea to find a moisturizer with SPF protection and use it regularly. For max protection, apply sunscreen at least 20 minutes before you head out the door to give it time to soak in.

If you must have the sun-bronzed look for summer, try a fake bake. The new self-tanners don't turn you freak orange like the old ones did. Products like Coppertone Endless Summer Sunless Tanning Lotion is about ten bucks and leaves your skin "sun-kissed" yet safe. Of course, the trick is applying the stuff evenly, so you might want to recruit a pal to help.

Q. How do I take care of my skin when my face is oily, my legs are flaky, and it seems to change every day!?

A. Great question. Welcome to "combination skin," what happens as you hit puberty and your pores begin pumping out more oil on some parts of your bod—like your back and face—but not on others, like your arms and legs. Because your facial skin tends to be most sensitive, it's best to give it special care with specific facial-cleansing products. (See Acne, page 2 for more info.) On the remaining fifteen or sixteen square feet of your skin, use a nonsoap liquid cleanser like Dove moisturizing wash that doesn't contain a lot of harsh chemicals. Those poofy nylon scrubbies are nice for cleaning your body because they help rub off dead skin cells without being too rough. And although showering feels great, it's not great for your skin to stand there for a half hour. Keep the water warm, but not hot, and make your shower as brief as possible.

Washing your skin daily is the best way to combat the oily stuff. Moisturizing it will help stop any dryness. Immediately after you step out of the shower, apply a moisturizing lotion. Your skin will be healthiest overall if you exercise, eat right, and get a full night's sleep regularly.

Q. What are these bumps?

A. Going to school puts you in contact with a *lot* of people, which means *tons* of opportunities to come in contact with fungi, bacteria, and viruses that give you itchy, red rashes. You can also get rashes from everyday stuff like dyes from your new favorite shirt; too much time in the sun; plants like poison ivy; soaps, lotions, and detergents; metal jewelry; even something you ate if you're allergic to it. And your body chemistry changes, so even if you were never allergic to something before, you can have a reaction now. In most cases, the rashes will go away on their own, or with the help of a little medicated lotion. Sometimes, however, you may need to see a doctor. Sometimes rashes are from medical conditions, and you'll need to learn how to treat them and how to keep them from coming back. Others require special meds you can only get from a doctor. Whatever it is that's causing your itch, the basic advice is the same—don't scratch! Show your mom and dad and keep an eye on it while you're treating it to be sure it doesn't spread.

Skin

Since rashes can be pretty gross, your best bet is to try to avoid them. Though you can't totally rash-proof your bod, there are some smart steps you can take. Mainly, steer clear of stuff you *know* can irritate your skin, like harsh soaps and poisonous plants; wash your clothes before you wear them; and keep your skin clean.

"I don't mind the usual self-care stuff like brushing my teeth or showering, but I sometimes get annoyed with the new stuff I have to do, like putting on deodorant and washing my face with special cleansers, and using skin lotions and creams."

Liz, 13

Q. Why do I have so many freckles?

A. Everyone's skin contains a pigment called melanin. Some people have a lot of melanin, which makes their skin dark brown or black. Some have little melanin, so they look more light-skinned. Sometimes those pigment cells clump together, and you have freckles. If you're freckle-prone, you get more of these little reddish-brown dots when you're in the sun. This is because sunlight triggers melanin-producing cells to crank out more of the pigment, which can cause more freckles to crop up on your face, arms, chest, and other exposed skin. Freckles are nothing to fret over, though. Most folks think they're cute.

Q. I have stretch marks on my legs. How can I get rid of them?

A. That means you're growing, girl! Sometimes when you grow really fast, your skin can't keep up and you end up with a purplish or whitish line. These can show up on your legs, breasts, and hips especially. Don't stress. Often they fade with time. You can help erase them with lotions that contain glycolic acid. It's also a good idea to eat a healthy diet full of fruits and vegetables that contain vitamin C, like oranges, tomatoes, and leafy green veggies, because C helps you produce the collagen you need to produce healthy skin.

Q. Why do I turn red when I'm embarrassed?

A. You have thousands of tiny blood vessels in your skin. When you get embarrassed, your heart beats faster and fills those vessels with blood, turning you a pretty shade of pink. But don't sweat it, everyone blushes. Take a few deep breaths and move on.

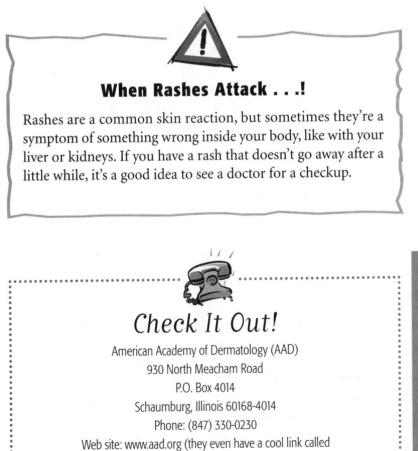

When Rashes Attack . . .!

Rashes are a common skin reaction, but sometimes they're a symptom of something wrong inside your body, like with your liver or kidneys. If you have a rash that doesn't go away after a little while, it's a good idea to see a doctor for a checkup.

Check It Out!

American Academy of Dermatology (AAD)
930 North Meacham Road
P.O. Box 4014
Schaumburg, Illinois 60168-4014
Phone: (847) 330-0230
Web site: www.aad.org (they even have a cool link called
"Kid's Connection" for preteens and adolescents)

Skin

Teeth

Grin and Bare 'Em!

Once you've passed the age of scoring pocket change for pearly whites left under your pillow, the teeth you see when you flash a smile at the mirror are the ones you'll have forever. You have thirty-two teeth total—all different sizes and shapes to help you bite, chew, and talk. Since they're the only ones you've got, it's important to develop good dental habits now—during your cavity-prone years—to keep those choppers healthy and white for the rest of your life. Here's what you need to know.

Q. What causes cavities and how can I prevent them?

A. Germs, girlfriend. It works like this: Your mouth is crawling with bacteria—not something to get grossed out about, just a fact of life. The sticky film known as plaque that you see on your teeth sometimes is where these germs live. Many of the foods you eat cause these bacteria to produce acids. It's these acids that dissolve the enamel that protects your teeth, which leads to holes in the enamel, better known as cavities. Left untreated, a cavity turns into a painful toothache because the sensitive root of your tooth, which is usually protected, is exposed through the hole. That's why it's important to have your teeth cleaned and checked twice a year.

Brushing and flossing are the two biggest actions you can take against cavities. You should brush at least twice a day—in the morning and before bed—and floss once a day to get all the stuff out from between your teeth. If you get more cavities than you think you should, you also might want to use a germ-killing mouthwash, like Listerine. It's a little strong, but today's flavors aren't as mediciney tasting as they used to be.

Being prone to cavities also can run in the family. If your mom or dad has a mouth full of fillings, your enamel may be naturally a little softer. That's why some girls brush their teeth faithfully and still end up with cavities, while others are a little more slack and still manage to be cavity-free. But if you fall into the first group, you don't have to be doomed to a future of drilling and filling. Your dentist can apply something known as a sealant on your teeth. A sealant is a protective barrier applied to your teeth—usually to your back teeth because they're the most cavity prone—to protect them from decay. It's a totally painless procedure and pretty common among kids ages six to fourteen, when cavities strike most. But remember, just because you have the protection of a sealant doesn't mean you don't have to brush or floss!

"I used to wear braces, and I didn't like them that much. I was happy at first, because I knew that they would make my teeth look better, but after that they were kind of annoying. Food got stuck in them and I had to go to my orthodontist at least once a month, sometimes more if a wire or other part of my braces broke."

Liz, 13

Q. Does candy really rot your teeth?

A. Rot is a pretty strong word. But there's no question that certain foods contribute more to tooth decay than others. While all sugary foods can be a problem, the sticky stuff like caramel and taffy and even otherwise healthful foods like raisins are the worst because they cling to the crevices of your teeth. They take hours to completely dissolve, and all the while the germs in your mouth are pumping out acid. Surprisingly, foods like breads and potato chips can also cause cavities. They also tend to stick to your teeth, and because they're starchy (that is, full of carbohydrates), they turn into acid-producing sugar. And soda can deliver a *double* whammy to your tooth enamel. For one, it's sugary, and you know that's a problem. But all sodas—even sugar-free diet kinds—are way acidic. So drinking a lot of soda is like giving your teeth an acid bath every day, and that kind of bath can definitely cause wear!

Of course, no one is going to stop eating sweets or drinking soda altogether. What you can do is choose nutritious foods as often as possible, and when you do feel like something sweet or snacky, make a point of washing it down with plenty of water, swishing it over your teeth before you swallow to dilute the acid and wash it away. Limiting the number of times you snack each day can help, too. Remember that every time you eat something, the germs produce acid for about twenty minutes. So if you snack ten times a day, your teeth are being bathed in acid for more than three hours! Better to have three good meals and a couple snacks washed down with plenty of H_2O.

Q. If my teeth are crooked, does that mean I'll need braces?

A. Not necessarily. You lose your baby teeth and they're replaced with permanent teeth one at a time as your jaw grows and makes room for all those big new teeth. Sometimes, though, your new teeth come in before your jaw is done growing, and your teeth can be a little bunched up in there. If that's the case, your jaw might grow enough for your teeth to "unbunch" and straighten out. Also, just because your teeth are not perfectly straight doesn't mean they don't work just fine. Some people get braces simply because they want straight teeth. Others are perfectly happy with a little dental imperfection. Even Madonna has a gap between her front teeth, and she's certainly not shy about smiling for the cameras. In the end, getting braces for cosmetic reasons is a totally personal decision you need to talk over with your parents.

Sometimes, of course, girls need braces for more than cosmetic reasons. They may need to fix a jaw or bite problem. If you do need braces, don't feel bad! Millions of girls—and even plenty of grown-up women—wear braces. They're a temporary sacrifice to have a healthy, dazzling smile for the rest of your life. They'll be off before you know it! But you do need to take some special care while you're wearing them to avoid problems:

- **Brush carefully, and floss, too.** It's especially important to clean your teeth carefully when you have braces so you don't develop tooth decay where the braces sit. Ask your dentist what's the best brush to use—there are special brushes that make access to tight nooks and crannies easier—and be sure to brush after you eat, every single time. Flossing may be a little trickier with brackets and wires on your teeth, but, like brushing, it's even more important now. Have your dentist show you how.

- **Choose smart snacks.** Let's just say that candy-coated apples are not the best snack choice for a girl who has braces. Sticky, gummy candies can get trapped in your braces, which can be a dental disaster. Biting into hard foods can damage your braces. Better to cut tough stuff like apples, pears, and carrots into bite-sized morsels to just pop in your mouth.

Q. What's the best way to brush?

A. The best way to brush is in a circular motion, making little ovals with your brush, rather than just going up and down or back and forth. Brushing just straight back and forth can actually wear away at your teeth, which won't hurt now, but could leave them feeling sensitive by the time you're an adult. Remember to brush *all* the surfaces of your teeth, not just the ones you see. First brush the chewing surfaces of your teeth. This helps to soften the bristles before brushing other areas, especially near the gums, which can be sensitive. Then brush the fronts of your teeth, the parts people see. And finally, angle the brush and clean the backs of all your teeth. Oh, and don't forget your tongue—giving it a quick brush helps clean off germs that can contribute to bad breath. Use a soft bristled brush and be sure the head of the brush is small enough to fit comfortably in your mouth. And remember—spit out, never swallow, toothpaste.

"I've had braces for about five months. They're the metal ones. Once you get used to them, they're okay, but they were kind of uncomfortable at first. It was hard getting used to eating, and I was worried about breaking them."

Kortni, 10

Q. Do I really need to floss?

A. Yep! You know how popcorn and corn kernels can get stuck between your teeth? Well they're not the only things that get caught in there. Bits of *everything,* from bread to fruit, can get trapped in the tight spaces between your teeth, causing decay. Flossing cleans out all that trapped food and also rubs away the sticky plaque. Try it—you'll be surprised how much gunky stuff is in there! Flossing takes a little practice, but according to Dr. Barbara Rich, spokesperson for Academy of General Dentistry, it's not hard to do. Just follow these steps:

1. Tear off about a foot or so of floss.

2. Wind most of it around your right middle finger. Wind the remaining floss around the middle finger of your left hand, leaving a few inches of floss between your hands.

3. Hold the floss between your thumbs and forefingers.

4. Guide the floss between your teeth using a gentle sawing motion. Don't jam the floss between your teeth. You'll hit your gums and that hurts.

5. When the floss reaches your gums, curve the floss into a "C" shape against one tooth and slide it into the space between the tooth and gum.

6. Gently rub up on the side of the tooth, moving the floss away from the gum. Do this several times.

7. Clean all sides of your teeth using this technique.

8. Don't forget the backs of your very back teeth.

Q. How can I keep my teeth white?

A. The best way is to avoid the stuff that stains them. Forget about smoking! Aside from the fact that it makes your clothes and hair stink and it hurts your lungs so you can't hang on the soccer field, it turns your teeth a disgusting yellowish brown. Other staining stuff includes coffee, colas, and tea. Since you're not likely to avoid everything that dulls your teeth, seeing your dentist regularly for a good cleaning will help. Some people are born with teeth that are a little yellow or splotchy. Usually, you're the only one who notices, but if it really bothers you, it's possible to get them bleached. But only a dentist can do that. Stay away from bleaching kits you can buy at the drug store—you could end up doing more harm than good to your young teeth.

Teeth

Tell Your Dentist About Tender Gums!

Sometimes your gums may bleed a little when you floss, especially the first time, but this shouldn't happen a lot. And they shouldn't bleed when you brush your teeth. If your gums are red, swollen, or tender or they bleed when you brush, tell your parents and have them make an appointment with your dentist.

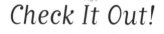

Check It Out!

American Dental Association
211 East Chicago Avenue
Chicago, Illinois 60611
Phone: (312) 440-2500
Web site: www.ada.org (has a special section just for kids and teens)

Academy of General Dentistry
Public Information Department
211 East Chicago Avenue, Suite 900
Chicago, Illinois 60611-2670
Phone: (312) 440-4300
Web site: www.agd.org

Vagina

The Ins and Outs of Your Reproductive Self

nlike guys, who refer to their sexual organs *way* too often, most girls rarely even utter the word vagina (pronounced vuh•JIGH•na) or any other slang term for it. In fact, it'll surprise you to know that you probably don't even really know what your vagina is! Though we all (adults, too) tend to call everything between our legs the vagina, there's really a lot more going on down there than meets the eye—literally. See, your vagina is actually *inside* your body, along with your reproductive organs. What's on the outside is your vulva. Though you may not talk about it often, it's still good to know what you've got going on there. So, finally, here are answers to all your "down there" questions, including some you maybe never even thought to ask.

Q. What are all these folds and bumps?

A. Because our sexual organs are positioned where we can't just bend over and see them, girls need a mirror and a little privacy to get a good look. So the first thing to do is grab a hand mirror and shut your door (tight—this is going to look mighty strange!). Then get comfortable and take a peek. Here's a guided tour, from the top down, of what you'll see (see figure 1):

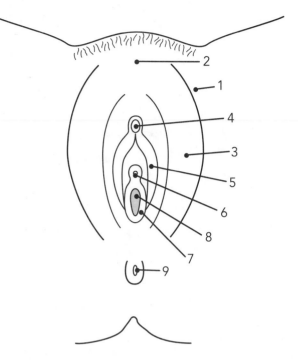

Figure 1. The parts of the outer vagina.

1. **Vulva.** The vulva is the technical name for all of your visible genitals, so everything you see in the mirror is your vulva.

2. **Mons** (mahnz). The raised mound of flesh over your pubic bone, where pubic hair eventually grows, is called the mons or "mound of Venus." It's a fleshy pad that protects this sensitive area.

3. **Outer lips or labia majora** (LAY·be·uh muh·JORE·uh). The outer lips are folds of skin that come together to protect the rest of the genitals. They're kind of like swinging doors to the vagina. You can open them with your fingers or by opening your legs. You will develop hair here as well.

4. **Clitoris** (pronounced both KLI·tuh·rus and kli·TOR·us). Peeking out beneath the spot where the outer lips meet at

the top is a pea-sized organ called the clitoris. Though you can only see the top, the clitoris has a shaft that extends into your body. It's filled with nerves and of all the parts of the vulva, it is the most sensitive to touch. Like a penis (but much smaller, of course), the clitoris swells in response to sexual feelings. This little organ helps women experience sexual pleasure and orgasm—a nice release of sexual tension that can follow sexual arousal. (See also Sexuality, page 133.)

5. **Inner lips or labia minora** (LAY•be•uh muh•NORE•uh). Nestled inside the outer lips, the inner lips are folds of hairless skin that provide additional protection for the genitals. They come together at the top, forming a little hood around the clitoris. Your inner lips may be very small or may be quite pronounced, even extending past the outer lips.

6. **Urethra** (yur•REE•thra). For the record, you don't pee out of your vagina. You pee out of a little hole, the urethra, that sits between your clitoris and your vaginal opening. This hole is part of a tube that runs to your bladder, so you can release urine when it's full.

7. **Vaginal** (VA•juh•nul or vuh•JIGH•nul) **opening.** Located below the urethra is your vaginal opening, a hole that's the opening to the canal that is your vagina, which leads to your internal reproductive organs. Though it looks mighty small, the vaginal opening is actually *extremely* elastic. It might seem impossible, but this is the place a fully developed baby, ready to be born, passes through!

8. **Hymen** (HIGH•min). If you peer into your vaginal opening, you *may* see a thin covering of skin, the hymen, partially blocking the entrance. Because menstrual blood needs a way out, the hymen doesn't completely cover the opening, but usually has one or more small openings in it. Some of you have a very distinct hymen, and some of you may have trouble locating it.

Vagina

9. **Anus** (AY•nis). Look way below your vaginal opening and you'll see your anus. It's not part of the vulva, but it's located in the same neighborhood. As you likely already know, this small hole is the opening to your rectum and colon, and it's where you pass solid wastes (bowel movements) out of your body. Because the anus is close to the vagina, it's important that when you wipe following a bowel movement you wipe away from your vaginal opening rather than toward it so you avoid getting nasty bacteria in there that can cause an infection.

Q. Where does my vagina go?

A. Your vagina is actually a muscular tube, or canal, that connects the outside of your body to your uterus and other reproductive organs inside your body. The canal's normal state is to be squeezed shut, so you won't be able to see in. But if you were to put a camera (and some lights!) inside your vagina, here's what you would see (see figure 2):

1. **Vaginal canal.** Your vagina is three to five inches in length, give or take (when you're fully grown). The walls are usually closed up against each other, and they are bumpy to the touch. The muscles that line the canal are strong and versatile. They can expand and contract to hold a tampon in place or to push out a baby.

2. **Cervix** (SIR•vicks). Between the uterus (see below) and the vagina is the cervix. The cervix is like the gatekeeper between the vagina and the uterus. It has a tiny opening, called the os (ohz), which means "orifice" or "mouth," in its center. The os allows menstrual blood out and sperm in (so eggs can get fertilized), and it prevents larger objects, like tampons, from passing through.

3. **Uterus** (YOU•ter•iss). This is the space where babies grow, also called the womb (pronounced woom). Along the sides is a lining, which cyclically each month becomes engorged (thick) with blood. This lining is where an egg im-

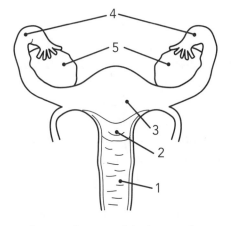

Figure 2. The parts of the inner vagina.

plants if it becomes fertilized and you become pregnant. This is also what sheds monthly when you are not pregnant and comes out as your "period." The uterus is fairly small, but can expand to many times its size to accommodate a baby.

4. **Fallopian** (full•OH•pee•un) **tubes.** Coming out of the top of the uterus on either side is a pair of channels about four inches long called the Fallopian tubes. They connect the inside of your uterus to your ovaries (see below). The ends of the tubes have fingerlike extensions that surround the ovaries, but aren't actually hooked to them. Each month, the Fallopian tubes carry a mature egg (called an ovum) from one of your ovaries and deliver it to the uterus.

5. **Ovaries** (OH•vir•eze). Connected to the uterus via the Fallopian tubes, these two lima bean–sized organs on each side of your uterus hold all the eggs (called ova, plural) you'll have for your entire life. Of course, your ova are totally tiny—put the tip of your pen on a piece of paper and twist. The mark you make is about the size of one egg.

Vagina

Q. Do all girls look the same down there?

A. Nope. Just as your breasts, eyes, and feet are slightly different from everyone else's, so are your sexual organs. Some girls have very pronounced lips and sexual organs, while others are smaller. Pubic hair comes in different shades and textures, too. What's more, your vulva changes as you grow into a mature woman. Your mons and outer and inner lips may get fleshier, the skin surrounding your vagina may get darker, and your clitoris may grow larger. All these changes can happen throughout puberty, so, depending on what stage of development you're in now, you may look very different a few years from now—or you may look much the same!

Q. Can I really tear my hymen horseback riding?

A. It sounds crazy, but yes. It's just a paper-thin layer of skin, and it can tear during vigorous sports, like bicycling, horseback riding, gymnastics, and soccer, or even if you take a bad spill. Occasionally, girls tear their hymen inserting or removing a tampon. If it remains intact into adulthood, the hymen will definitely get torn the first time you have sexual intercourse. Whenever the hymen breaks, you'll likely see some bright red blood afterward, which is why this barrier has been given the crude slang nickname the "cherry." (Sometimes you might hear rude jokes using that slang term—now you know that's what they're talking about.)

Q. I often have sticky stuff in my underwear. Is this normal?

A. As you may have noticed, your vagina is hardly dry. Like the inside of your mouth and nose, the vaginal walls are covered with a mucous membrane that produces moisture. This lubrication serves a lot of functions. For one, it keeps the vagina clean and helps prevent infections. It also carries out dead skin cells (your vagina sheds and generates cells just like your skin). Finally, vaginal moisture creates a slippery surface that helps women have sexual intercourse when they are ready. All this moisture and these secretions have to go somewhere, so they come out and end up on your underwear. How much discharge you have varies from day to day, but it's perfectly normal to have a clear and smooth or creamy, slightly gooey discharge that looks crusty when it dries. What you shouldn't see is funky colored, greenish or yellowish discharge, especially if it also smells bad and makes you itch like crazy—that's a sign of infection. Discharge also can be a symptom of infection if it's very thick and lumpy (think cottage cheese) and you feel burning or pain when you pee. If you have any of these symptoms, you need to tell your mom so she can make an appointment with a doctor to get it taken care of.

Q. What should I do if my vagina smells bad?

A. As mentioned above, if you have unusual discharge and a bad odor, you may have a vaginal infection that a doctor can treat with some simple medications. (Don't be embarrassed! Your doctor sees a lot of these and won't look at you funny at all.) Even if you don't have a discharge but you notice a fishy or otherwise strong smell down there—and you've washed carefully—it's best to get it checked out for hidden problems. Again, any conditions can usually be taken care of easily, but it's important to get the right treatment as soon as you notice a problem.

Otherwise, simple hygiene should keep your vagina clean and odorless. When washing your vulva, clean between all the lips and inside the folds, too, since sometimes toilet tissue or little bits of lint from your underwear can get trapped in there. Use an antibacterial wipe, like a baby wipe, if you detect a slight odor—it could just be the vaginal fluid mixing with the bacteria on your skin. And don't worry too much if you have a slight musky odor after exercising. We all smell a little when we sweat! Just be sure not to sit around in sweaty shorts. And change into clean cotton underwear (or at least underwear with a cotton lining) every day. Cotton lets your body breathe, so moisture doesn't get trapped in there and cause dampness, odor, and maybe irritation or even infection.

Vagina

Q. What is douching (DOO·shing)? Should I do it?

A. Douching involves squirting some type of solution, chemical or natural, into your vagina. Women have traditionally douched to smell "fresher," but it's really not a good idea. You have a delicate chemical balance in your vagina that douching can wreck, leaving you more susceptible to infections. It also can spread existing infections. Worse, douching actually can drive new bacteria into your vagina and cervix, creating problems you otherwise wouldn't have had.

Peeing Should Be Painless!

If it ever burns or hurts when you urinate, if you have blood in your urine, or if it seems like you have to go every five minutes, you might have a urinary tract infection (UTI). They're fairly common in women, and your doctor can clear it up with antibiotics you take in the form of a pill. You can help prevent UTIs by drinking plenty of water and wiping front to back after using the bathroom. Drinking cranberry juice can help, too.

Check It Out!

American College of Obstetrics and Gynecology (ACOG)
409 12th Street, S.W.
Washington, D.C. 20090-6920
Phone: (202) 638-5577
Web site: www.acog.com

Weight

Shaping a Beautiful New You

Let's say it right up front: A lot of girls are uncomfortable discussing their weight, especially gaining weight. Bombarded with messages on television and in magazines about how great it is to lose weight, girls get scared that gaining weight is a bad thing. Studies show that almost 65 percent of middle-school–age girls worry about their weight sometimes. But listen up—all those weight-loss ads and diet messages are designed for people much, much older than you— *not* for girls going through puberty! Now is the time when you're turning into an adult. It's only natural—and healthy and attractive— as you grow taller by leaps and bounds that you're going to gain some weight, too, to fill out your new figure. That's something to celebrate, not be scared about. Here's more on the shape of the new you.

"When I turned twelve, I put on a lot of weight all at once. I hated how it made me feel awkward, and I couldn't run as fast. But my mom told me that it was just a phase that all girls go through and I'd grow into it. She was right."

Christie, 13

Q. How much should I weigh?

A. Tough question! How much you should weigh depends on a lot of things: how old you are, how tall you are, how far through puberty you are, and how muscular you are, just to name a few. The range of weight considered "normal" at this time in your life is pretty big because your body is growing and changing so quickly. If your weight is really worrying you, talk to your mom about making an appointment with your doctor. He or she will be able to tell you for sure if you have anything to be concerned about. Your family doctor also can give you advice for keeping your weight healthy and normal all your life.

Q. I've gained ten pounds in the past year! Is that normal??

A. You bet! It's not uncommon for girls your age to add four inches in height in one year, so it's equally normal that you would put on ten pounds, and maybe more, to go with that added height. Throughout her growing spurt, it's not uncommon for a girl to gain forty pounds or more. Remember, we're not talking about "getting fat" here. We're talking about developing breasts (they count toward your weight, too!) and hips; putting on lean, strong muscle; and growing longer, stronger bones. Even your internal organs are growing! All that adds up, so it's very important that you don't look at the increasing number on the scale and just think "fat!" It's all of you transforming from kid to young adult.

Q. My mom and dad are both overweight. Does that mean I will be too?

A. Good question. We know now that some weight problems are hereditary, meaning that they run in families. So it's good to be aware. But you don't need to be excessively worried. Just because your mom and dad have problems with their weight doesn't necessarily mean you will, too. The best strategy is to use common sense when you eat (which is what everyone should do anyway) and try to choose mostly healthful, nutritious foods. If you eat mostly fruits and veggies, whole grains, and other healthful foods (see Nutrition, page 208) and just a few snack foods like chips, cakes, sodas, and cookies, you should be just fine. An even better idea: Ask your parents to join you in your healthful eating campaign. That way you can all feel good together.

Q. I keep hearing about how so many kids have weight problems. How can I make sure I stay within the normal weight range?

A. Stay active! Here's the scoop: You're right, there is a lot of talk these days about kids and weight. Problem is, many kids today are much, much less active than kids used to be. Computers, television, and video games have replaced going outside to play for a lot of kids. That means they're not getting the exercise they need. Plus, it's supereasy to munch away on tons of junk food when you're plopped in front of the television playing PlayStation. The result is that many more kids than in the past are developing weight problems, which sets them up for weight and other health problems when they grow up. The good news is that kids can totally turn this trend around. All you have to do is turn off the computer and the television, grab a ball or a bike, and head outside! Studies show that when kids play sports, they have healthier bodies, they feel better about their bodies, and they're more likely to grow up into healthy, active adults. And that's all good.

"I've noticed that I've been eating a lot more lately and have gained much more weight than I've gained in the past, but I'm comfortable with these changes. I'm still thin."

Liz, 13

Q. My friend and I both play the same sports and eat the same foods. Yet, she's much skinnier than I am. Why?

A. You may have different body types. Take a look around your school or the mall and you'll see that people are built dozens of

Weight

different ways. Some people are short and muscular; some are tall and lanky. Some have fuller breasts, some have smaller breasts. Legs, hips, feet, and fingers—there are as many different shapes and sizes as there are people. If you're designed to be curvier or more muscular, that's the way your body is going to be—and that's okay! Remember, too, that your friend may be at a different stage of puberty than you are, so she might not be done filling out yet. Whatever the case, it doesn't matter. You each have your own special, unique body. And what's most important is that you're active and healthy.

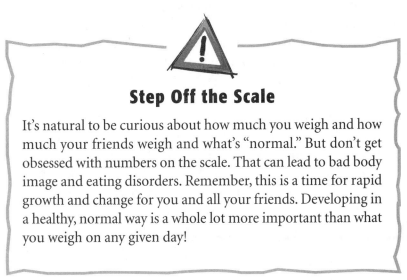

Step Off the Scale

It's natural to be curious about how much you weigh and how much your friends weigh and what's "normal." But don't get obsessed with numbers on the scale. That can lead to bad body image and eating disorders. Remember, this is a time for rapid growth and change for you and all your friends. Developing in a healthy, normal way is a whole lot more important than what you weigh on any given day!

Check It Out!

American Academy of Pediatrics
141 Northwest Point Boulevard
Elk Grove Village, Illinois 60007-1098
Phone: (847) 434-4000
Web site: www.aap.org

Weight

confidence

crushes

Part Two

hormones

Will I Ever Feel

Normal?

intelligence

moods

period PMS

sexuality

stress

well-being

Confidence
Hold Your Head High

Studies show that girls' confidence—or how much they believe in their abilities—is pretty high . . . right up 'til they start hitting puberty. That's the time when a lot of girls start feeling a little more unsure of themselves and their confidence gets shaky. This is understandable when you consider all the changes you're going through. Dealing with a body that looks different from one day to the next, new emotions that erupt out of the blue, and learning a whole new world of tampons, pads, and bras can make even the most confident girl want to crawl into her shell now and then. But let's face it: Spending your life with your head in the sand is a drag. And confidence is way important for reaching your goals and feeling good about yourself. Here's how to keep that head held high—even through the toughest times.

Q. I get good grades, but I don't feel confident in the classroom, especially when the teacher calls on me. I just want to hide in the back. What can I do?

A. You are not alone, girl! According to "Teens Before Their Time" research from the Girl Scouts, almost two-thirds of eight- to twelve-year-old girls surveyed admitted that they "never" or "sometimes don't" speak out in class because they're afraid of making "stupid" or "wrong" comments. It's natural to feel shy speaking out in front of others. Even many adults avoid it! But in classes, especially when class participation counts as part of your grade, it's important to overcome that fear and raise your hand. The best way to feel more confident in the classroom is to come into class prepared. If you read your lessons and stay on top of your homework, you have a better chance of answering the teacher's questions right, or at least very close, close enough that it shows you do know something about the topic. And if you get something wrong, so what? If some kid laughs or taunts you, shrug your shoulders and say "At least I'm not afraid to try" because it's true! And also, showing that kind of confidence has a way of putting teasers and bullies in their place.

Q. I'm afraid if I speak up too much my friends won't like me. Isn't it better to have friends?

A. Friends are one of the most important things in life, there's no doubt! But the great thing about real friends is that they don't stop being your friend just because they don't agree with something you said or because you raise your hand in third period history class. Having confidence in your friendships means that you know your friends will be there no matter what and that you'll be able to work out any minor differences you have. The best friends in life are the ones that help you grow into the great, competent girl you're becoming. And remember, you can always help your friends feel more confident, too, by encouraging them to speak up and be themselves.

Q. My best friend is perfect, pretty, athletic, super popular, and all the boys love her. I like her and everything, but what should I do when I feel so inferior around her?

A. It can be so hard to keep your own confidence intact when you're around someone who seems to be able to do it all effortlessly. But believe it or not, that girl has days when she feels unsure, too. And there are probably plenty of things she wishes she could do better. What's more, there are probably things you excel at, too. You just don't notice them as much because you're so busy comparing yourself to her!

One of the best things to do when you're feeling low on the self-confidence scale is remember something you like to do and do pretty well. Maybe you create killer designs for jewelry or you write awesome poetry or you like to sing. Learning a new skill also is a great confidence builder. Try something you've never done, like Rollerblading, snowboarding, or painting. You might be surprised to find a new skill you kick butt at. And even if you don't, you always gain confidence by having the courage to try new things. Another great confidence builder: volunteering! Talk to your parents about wanting to volunteer in your community, then check the newspapers for organizations looking for help. In helping people less fortunate than you, you can gain more confidence in your own abilities.

"The best part about being a girl is that you're more talented at most stuff, besides sports."

Samantha, 9

Q. I feel confident until I get around a bunch of boys. Then I just clam up. What's wrong with me?

A. Nothing is wrong with you. A whole lot of girls get shy in front of boys. As you become more aware of boys, you become more concerned with what they think. As a result, you zip your lips because you're suddenly afraid of turning boys off or having them criticize you. The kicker is, boys like girls who aren't afraid to be themselves. Sure they tease sometimes. But they tease each other, too. If the teasing isn't mean, it may just be their way of playing around. Still, a lot of you feel intimidated when you're around a bunch of boys and that can be a hard feeling to shake. You might want to try finding an all-girl organization like a local Girl Scouts chapter or other local girls club where you can spend time being around just girls doing girl things. These organizations give you a chance to grow and explore who you are and what you're good at without worrying about boys. They're also great confidence builders because as a group, you get to decide many of the new things you'd like to try. You can go winter camping, canoeing, skiing, even rock climbing in a safe, totally supportive environment. Being able to take control of your life and try new and exciting things is where true confidence comes from.

Confidence Is Healthy!

Everyone feels unconfident sometimes. If you felt superconfident all the time that would mean you thought you were so perfect you could never fail. But while it's normal to feel nervous or have low confidence once in a while, especially before doing something new or taking a hard test, having zero confidence all the time isn't. If every day is a challenge for you, talk to your parents or a trusted adult, like a counselor. They (or someone they can lead you to) can help you find out why your confidence is in the dumps and help you lift it up where it belongs.

Check It Out!

Web site: jfg.girlscouts.org (Girl Scout–sponsored site just for girls and is a place where girls can speak out, get involved, and boost their confidence; helps you explore your thoughts on the world around you; you can talk about everything, including world issues, everyday challenges, favorite books, and even boys)

Crushes

Rehearsal for the Real Thing

The changes that happen during puberty are more than just physical. They're emotional, too. Crushes, for example, can be major, emotional experiences. Crushes are romantic or sexual feelings toward someone. They can be passing and mild to long-lasting and intense. Though they can feel like love, crushes really aren't the big L word. They're more like a dress rehearsal for love. Crushes are a safe way to explore what you like romantically, to learn what you would say to someone you really, really like, and to understand how sexual interests make you feel. Here's some questions girls commonly have about crushes.

Q. I'm nine and have this huge crush on this boy at school. My mom says I'm too young. I say I can't help how I feel. Who's right?

A. This is a totally common scenario. And it's not about figuring out who's right or wrong. You both know how you feel. The trick here is trying to understand one another. Your mom is likely concerned about you getting too serious about boys too soon, because you'll miss out on doing important stuff for yourself like developing hobbies, finding interests, and all the other things that girls who aren't focused on boys do. That said, no, you can't help having crushes. Nor should you. Having crushes is a normal, healthy part of growing up. And they're fun! Maybe you just need to reassure your mom that you're not so crazy obsessed about this boy that you're neglecting school, hobbies, friends, and, most important, yourself!

"I have crushes on boys, but I also like just being friends with them. Boys are sort of a big thing to me, but I never want to change just because a boy would like me better that way."

Tara, 13

Q. How do I know if someone I have a crush on likes me, too?

A. There are a lot of ways you can sort of tell if someone likes you. Does that person spend a lot of time talking to you? Do they seem to find reasons to be around you? Do they go out of their way to start conversations with you? If so, there's a good chance they like you, too. But there's really only one way to know for sure, and that's to ask! You don't have to ask directly "Do you like me?" (though you can). You can ask him to dance at the next dance. Or see if he wants to go to a special event with you. Another way to find out if someone likes you is to have a friend ask him for you. But be careful with this technique. Your friend may make a bigger deal out of it to the person than you want her to. Or she may not be as discreet as you'd like her to be, so the whole class will end up knowing about your crush when you wanted to keep it private. Though a really smooth pal can find out if someone likes you without making a huge production out of it or spilling the beans to the whole world, it's usually better to do this stuff on your own.

Q. I have a crush on my English teacher. Is it normal to like someone so much older?

A. Sure is! Many girls have their first crushes on a teacher, just like girls also have crushes on singers, movie stars, and television celebrities—all usually considerably older. Having a crush on someone much older—and maybe someone like a rock star, who you'll never even meet—is a safe way to explore sexual feelings without getting in too deep. The key to these crushes is enjoying them for what they're worth, but realizing that they're unattainable and not getting too carried away with them. It's fun to pretend now and then, but it's not healthy to invest a whole lot of heavy emotions in a fantasy romance.

"I have had so many crushes on boys! But I don't want to share too much about that."

Ashlyn, 13

Q. My friends told a boy I like that I had a crush on him, but he doesn't like me. Now I'm totally embarrassed and bummed out. What should I do?

A. You've just learned why they're called crushes! It's *never* easy to find out someone doesn't feel the same way about you as you feel about them. But don't let it devastate you or make you feel bad about yourself. Just because a particular boy doesn't have romantic feelings for you doesn't mean there's anything wrong with you. It just means that you're not his romantic type. Just like there are plenty of guys who you think are great friends but don't feel "that way" about. About feeling embarrassed, that will pass. Just act yourself around the boy and don't make a big deal of it. Chances are he won't either. (He probably feels embarrassed, too.) And tell your friends to keep your crushes quiet from now on or you won't be sharing your secrets with them. If you still feel very upset, try talking to a trusted adult about how you're feeling. Sometimes it helps to talk it out, and chances are they'll have some similar stories from their own childhood, so you'll know you're not alone and you'll definitely get through this.

Q. I met a boy on the Internet and now have a huge crush on him. We chat every night, and I'd like to meet him. But I'm nervous. What should I do with this on-line crush?

A. Meeting someone online can feel cool and exciting. You can chat for hours, because it's so much easier to say things in e-mails and instant messages than it is to say them in person. You may also feel more relaxed and free to be yourself while hiding behind a computer. Problem is: It's also easier to be someone you're not—something that happens all too often online. Though that boy could be on the up and up, there's a chance he's not what he says he is. He could be a forty-year-old creepy man or a twenty-year-old druggy looking for cheap thrills. These kinds of guys can—and do—hide out on the Internet, pretending to be young cute guys so they can lure in girls. That's why it's never safe to give someone personal information about yourself, like where you live or your phone number, to someone you meet online. It's also not safe to meet them somewhere, as you could find yourself in a dangerous situation. The best thing to do is break off this romance and stick to meeting guys you can see for yourself. If the Internet crush keeps contacting you or if you think you've already told him too much about yourself, get a parent involved, pronto. Your mom or dad can respond to him and keep this from becoming a risky situation.

Crushes

Beware of Boy Obsession!

It's common for girls your age to be a little "boy crazy." But don't forget there's more to life than boys! Music videos, movies, and television shows can make you feel like you're a big lame-o if you don't have a boyfriend. But there's nothing further from the truth. In order to find out who you really are, what you like, and what you're good at, you need to spend time developing yourself without worrying what this boy or that boy thinks about you. Besides, you don't want all your self-worth wrapped up in what guys think, do you? Be sure to spend plenty of time with yourself and in all-girl activities like sports and a girls club so you can be yourself without getting distracted by boys.

Check It Out!

Web site: jfg.girlscouts.org (Girl Scout site that's about a whole lot more than badges. Find out about science; careers; and yes, boys. Psychology expert "Dr. M" and her daughter Liz answer all kinds of questions about crushes and relationships in their special "Girl Talk" area of the site.)

Crushes

Hormones

Welcome to Puberty!

As you go through puberty, there are tons of changes you can practically see happening right before your eyes. You grow breasts. Your hips get wider. You develop body hair. You get your first period. Behind all these visible changes, however, is a whirlwind of activity going on *inside* you that you can't see. The most important of these inner changes is the influx of hormones that are hard at work changing you from a girl to a young woman. These hormones trigger the start of puberty and are what will eventually help you get pregnant and have a baby. But *that's* obviously down the line a ways! Here's what you should know about hormones now.

"Sometimes all these new changes surprise me. New and weird things seem to be happening to me every day."

Ashlyn, 13

Q. What are hormones and what do they do?

A. Hormones are chemicals that your body produces. These chemicals travel through your bloodstream and tell different organs what to do. Though these chemicals affect much of your body in a major way, causing body hair, breast development, menstruation, acne, and all those other puberty changes, they actually begin in your head, specifically, in a gland at the base of your brain called the pituitary (puh•TOO•uh•tare•ee) gland. When the pituitary gland sends hormones to your ovaries, for example, they get the message that it's time to start producing more estrogen (a female hormone), which, among other things, helps start and control the menstrual cycle.

Once your hormones get rolling, typically between the ages of eight and eleven, puberty is on the way. Puberty happens gradually, in about five stages. These stages happen differently and at different times for everyone. What your best friend is going through won't necessarily be the same as what you're going through, so you won't be able to run around pronouncing, "I'm in stage three of puberty!" Stage one of puberty starts before you even know it, when your pituitary gland sends out the hormones that signal your ovaries (the reproductive organs that produce your eggs; see Vagina, page 77) that it's time to begin to grow and produce the necessary hormones for ovulation (the release of a ripe egg from your ovaries that eventually leads to menstruation; see Period, page 115). As your hormone levels rise and the hormones start working in your body, you go into stage two of puberty. This is when you notice that your breasts are beginning to develop. You'll see pubic hair starting to sprout, and you'll probably have a growth spurt. During stages three and four, your breasts continue developing and your pubic hair becomes thicker and begins forming a triangle on your mons. You'll notice hair under your arms and maybe on other parts of your body. Also during stages three and four, your hips will widen and you'll get your first period. Stage five of puberty is the end of this cascade of change. Your breasts are fully developed. Your periods are coming regularly. And you've reached maximum height.

The whole puberty process usually lasts three to five years, and once it's done, you're technically a woman, although there's no doubt you have a lot of growing up left to do before you can really feel like one! From this point, you'll have a nice stable flow of hormones until sometime in your thirties and forties, when your hormones will start to change again and your body gets ready to stop having periods, a stage called menopause.

(See Period, page 115 for more on hormones and menstruation.)

"School doesn't really prepare you for all the changes you go through. I've learned a lot from my mom and from reading body books."

Liz, 13

Q. How are girls' hormones different from boys' hormones?

A. Boys and girls actually produce the same hormones, just in very different amounts. Obviously, boys don't get a period, and girls don't have to worry about developing sperm (the tadpole-like creatures that fertilize a woman's eggs during sexual intercourse). Nobody has to tell you that boys and girls *look* totally different, too. You and your friends don't have facial whiskers. And boys don't need sports bras. All these differences can be attributed to our major "gender- and sex-related hormones," estrogen and testosterone. Though there are many other hormones hard at work in both boys and girls, estrogen is the primary female hormone and testosterone is the primary male hormone. Like girls, boys start puberty when their pituitary gland releases the chemicals that trigger the production of hormones. As you may have already noticed, boys usually go through puberty a couple years later than girls do. But don't worry, they'll catch up—and it can be just as exciting, strange, and awkward for them as it is for you.

Q. Why do some girls start puberty earlier or later than others?

A. Nobody knows for sure. We do know that some of it can be attributed to genetics. That is, if your mom started puberty at age nine, chances are you'll start around then, too. But there's more to it than that. Remember how puberty starts in your pituitary gland? Well, that gland is very sensitive to changes in your body. And when you reach a certain body weight, it "wakes up" and starts sending the signals to let puberty begin. That weight is different for everybody (again, that probably runs in your family). Some researchers have noticed that many girls are starting to enter puberty earlier today than they did years ago, but nobody quite knows why. It could be because good nutrition is letting us grow faster than we ever did. It could be that many children are heavier earlier than they used to be. Or it could be due to a whole bunch of different factors. But even if some girls are sprouting breasts earlier than they used to, the one big sign of puberty that hasn't budged in forty years is menstruation. The average girl still gets her first period when she's about twelve years old, though a few years earlier or later is normal, too. If you eat a healthful diet, exercise regularly, and take care of yourself, chances are you'll go through a well-timed, healthy puberty.

"All these puberty changes are kind of weird at first, but it gets better as you get used to it."

Britany, 11

Q. How else do hormones affect me?

A. All kinds of ways! Hormones trigger *all* those physical changes that puberty brings. You can thank (or blame!) all kinds of stuff—like breast development, body hair, acne, body odor, and menstruation—on your changing hormones. Hormones also affect more than the physical changes going on outside and inside your body. They affect how you feel. Changes in your moods are often related to changes in your hormones, which is why you may feel bouncy one day and kind of down the next even though nothing has happened that might make

Hormones

you feel happier or sadder or grumpier. As your hormones change, you'll also start having sexual feelings. Hormones like testosterone (remember, girls have it too) and progesterone (one of the hormones involved in menstruation) make you look at boys in a whole new, and often exciting, way. Some of you might be embarrassed by these sexual thoughts, but they are totally natural. Though you're a long way from being emotionally and psychologically mature enough to act on these feelings, it can be fun to notice boys and enjoy knowing that you're growing up!

Sometimes Hormones Need Help!

Hormonal changes happen at different rates for everyone, so don't sweat it too much if you're the only girl wearing a bra—or not wearing one—in your circle of friends. However, sometimes hormones can be a little out of whack. If you are in your mid-teens and still see no signs of puberty on the horizon—you haven't developed breasts or body hair, for instance—you should see a doctor to make sure your hormone levels are A-okay. Likewise, if you're very young, like six or seven, and you're galloping toward the bra department, you might want to get a quick checkup.

Hormones

Check It Out!

American Association of Clinical Endocrinologists
(an endocrinologist is a doctor who specializes in hormones)
1000 Riverside Avenue, Suite 205
Jacksonville, Florida 32204
Phone: (904) 353-7878
Web site: www.aace.com

American College of Obstetrics and Gynecology (ACOG)
409 12th Street, S.W.
Washington, D.C. 20090-6920
Phone: (202) 638-5577
Web site: www.acog.com

Intelligence

The Brains Behind the Operation

U sed to be, scientists thought your brain grew super fast 'til you were about five or six years old. Then, they said, that was it. No more gray matter growth. The brains you had in kindergarten had to last a lifetime. Now we know better. Today, scientists have shown that the same hormones that make you sprout hips and breasts also give you a boost between the ears! Starting around age ten to twelve, your mental powers pick up a second wind and your brain develops further through your teen years. That's why now is a perfect time to stimulate your "smarts" and make the most of your mental development. Here's what you need to know.

Q. What is IQ?

A. IQ is short for Intelligence Quotient. It's a number score, like 100, that is supposed to indicate your general brain power. You might have taken an IQ test in school. It's a standardized exam that measures different mental abilities, like spatial thinking and logical reasoning, rather than factual knowledge, like seeing if you know when the Revolutionary War was. Though no test can measure *all* of your brain's amazing capabilities, experts say that your IQ score is a decent predictor of how well you will perform at various academic tasks. It's really important to remember, however, that your IQ score is only a number. What's more important is how motivated and enthusiastic you are in school. A lot of people with an "average" IQ score have become successful doctors, lawyers, businesspeople, and professionals. Likewise, people with a genius-level IQ score don't always go on to professional stardom. And a lower IQ score doesn't necessarily mean you can't answer the same questions someone with a higher score answers; it might mean just that the person with the higher score may be able to answer the problem more quickly.

Q. Can I change my IQ?

A. Yes! Using your brain helps build your IQ. The more you read, explore, study, and pay attention in school, the better chance you have of adding a few points to your IQ score. Likewise, your IQ score can drop if you neglect your brain. Studies show that kids who drop out of school actually *lose* IQ points. So treat your brain like a muscle: Use it or lose it!

Q. Are boys really smarter than girls at math?

A. We've all heard the old adage: Boys are better at math, and girls are better at reading. We've heard it so much, maybe we've started to believe it. But it's not really true. In a recent study of 14,000 boys and girls from elementary to high school, researchers found that young girls actually tended to have *higher* math scores than boys. In high school, boys had very slightly higher scores—like 1.5 percent higher—on average. But that's hardly enough support to say that boys are smarter than girls in math. Some researchers in the past have found that boys tend to do slightly better in math on their SATs than girls do, but most teachers now say that boys and girls can do equally well in both math and verbal skills. What's important is that you don't let silly girl/boy stereotypes discourage you from trying!

Q. Does watching television really rot my brain?

A. Well, your brain probably won't turn to mush and start pouring out of your ears, but watching too much television is anything but good for you. For the most part, watching television is a passive experience—it does all the thinking for you while you turn your brain off and chill out. That's okay for a little bit, like after a tough day at school. But remember that use-it-or-lose-it stuff? Shut off your brain too long, and it won't be as sharp as it should be. Plus television doesn't encourage you to use your imagination—one of the coolest parts of your brain! The best bet: Pick one favorite show a day and limit yourself to that. Find better things to do with your brain—like reading, writing poetry, playing games—the rest of your relaxation time.

"Girls can challenge boys. I'm proud that I've been able to become president of my school. I'm the first girl president of my elementary school since they started it thirteen years ago."

Britany, 11

Q. Is it true that boys don't like "brainy" girls?

A. Now *there's* an old-fashioned stereotype! Boys like girls they can talk to—and that means she's got to have some pretty sharp gray matter under that hair of hers. If a boy makes fun of you for being a "brain," remember—that same boy probably makes fun of people for wearing glasses or for being short. He's probably the kind of person who needs to tease others to feel good about himself. Or maybe it's actually that he has a crush on you! Boys often tease girls to get their attention. Either way, don't ever let someone's teasing stunt your smarts. When the time comes, you'll find plenty of guys who think girls with brains are the best.

Q. How can I make my brain as smart as possible?

A. Challenge it! Do plenty of reading; pay attention in school; ask questions; imagine all the different, exciting things you want to do with your life. And keep your brain healthy. Like the rest of your body, your brain needs fresh air and good food. Feed it plenty of healthy stuff like fruits and vegetables, whole grains, and fish. Take it outside to play so it gets a lot of oxygen and fresh blood flowing into it. And make sure you give it plenty of rest, at least nine hours of sleep a night.

Don't Be Dumb!

One of the most important things to do for your developing brain is stay away from drugs and alcohol! Both can hurt your brain in ways that last your whole life. People who use ecstasy even for just a week or two can get brain damage that shows up seven years later. Marijuana damages your memory and mental abilities. And alcohol is known to destroy brain cells. In short, using alcohol and drugs is pretty stupid, so stay smart and don't do it!

Check It Out!

National Education Association
1201 Sixteenth Street N.W.
Washington, D.C. 20036
Phone: (202) 833-4000
Web site: www.nea.org

Moods
All the Emotions You Feel

You wake up feeling happy. By breakfast you're blue. You love your mom. Your mom makes you want to scream. Up and down, back and forth. Sometimes your moods make you wonder if you're losing your mind! Relax. You're not. You're simply on that roller coaster called the Puberty Express. The cost of admission is free—but it can get pretty wild. Here's what you need to know to hang on and enjoy the ride!

"My mood most days is happy."

Tara, 13

Q. Why do I sometimes feel angry or sad for no reason?

A. In a word: hormones. As you go through puberty, lots of hormones start surging through your body. Sometimes they all gush out at once, making you feel those sudden highs or lows. That's why you can be sunny one minute, stormy the next. Of course, there's plenty of other stuff affecting your moods, too.

As you grow up, you go through constant changes. Your body changes, your classrooms change, your friends change. All this adds up, and sometimes you can end up feeling restless or blue without really being able to say why, because it's not just one thing, it's the added effect of a bunch of things! It's all a normal, natural part of becoming a teenager and an adult.

Q. How can I help control my emotions?

A. You can't necessarily control when and how your emotions swing, but you *can* make yourself feel better when they dip into the down side. Here's a few tricks to make your moods more manageable:

- **Keep a journal.** When all your feelings are swirling around, take a minute to write them down. A lot of times just getting your feelings out by putting them down on paper can you make you feel calmer and more in control. Keeping a regular journal also gives you the chance to look back at your feelings from time to time and see what things tend to make you happy or sad.

- **Hug a pet.** Furry friends like cats and dogs are powerful mood lifters—even medical scientists say that snuggling or stroking a pet is a great way to beat the blues. If you have a pet, try giving him or her some love next time you're feeling low.

- **Run around!** Exercise actually stimulates brain chemicals that make you feel good. And there's no better way to blow off steam than going out for some play time.

- **Talk, talk, talk.** It's easy to clam up when you're not in the best of moods. But that is often the best time to open up. Talk to your mom or dad. Call a friend. Other people often can provide an outside prospective that will lift your spirits.

- **Volunteer.** Talk to your parents about helping with a volunteer organization. Little things like delivering groceries to a person who can't leave the house and playing basketball with disabled kids can make you feel better about yourself and help you realize how lucky you are.

Moods

Q. Sometimes I get so mad at my mom, I say things I don't mean. Then I feel worse. What can I do?

A. Everyone says things they don't mean sometimes; but remember that your mom has feelings, too, so it's good that you realize that you should try not to be mean, even when you're mad. Part of becoming an adult is learning how to talk calmly even through the stormiest feelings. The trick is being able to *explain* how you feel and why you feel that way rather than just blurting out "I hate you!" because you're angry about a decision your mom made or about something she said. For instance, if you ask your mom for permission to go to a concert and she says no, your first reaction might be to shout something mean, stomp upstairs, and slam the door. But that doesn't solve your problem. Instead, in fact, you added to your problems—you've said something you regret, your mom thinks you're having a temper tantrum, and you still aren't going to the concert. A better approach is to let your mom know how you feel and ask to talk about it. Say something like, "Mom, it makes me feel mad when you say no without hearing my side of the story. I feel like you don't even listen to me." Your mom still may say no. And you still may be mad that she won't let you go. But if you make it a point to communicate whenever you feel angry, your mom will have a better understanding of what you want to do and how you feel. Also, she may be more likely to negotiate a compromise with you when you talk calmly. What's more, you'll feel good about yourself, knowing you're in control, that you're behaving in a more mature manner.

Q. Lately when I'm with my friends, I just feel down. We used to have a lot in common. But now they all like doing stuff that I'm not interested in. Should I pretend I'm happy and go along with them to keep my friends?

Moods

A. No way! A major part of growing up is becoming your own person. Your interests will change many times as you get older, and so will some of your friends. Though it can be painful when friendships fade, ultimately you find new friends who share your new passions and interests. That doesn't mean you should just toss out old friends every time you get a new hobby. But if you no longer have much in common with your current group of pals and you're no longer happy, it's probably time to foster some new friendships. Of course this might happen the other way around, too. Maybe you and your best friend from two years ago used to love going to dance class together. Only, now she's not interested in dance anymore. She's taken up gymnastics. You may continue being friends. Or maybe you just won't hang out so much anymore. It's just a natural part of growing up, in fact, of life—it happens to adults, too. The most important thing to do is follow your heart.

"My mood most days is happy. But I do get moody."

Liz, 13

Q. Why don't parents understand what kids are feeling?

A. It's not really that your parents don't understand. It's that as grown-ups, they have been through a lot of what you're going through now, so they see things from that perspective. It's like if you were to listen to your younger brother or sister crying about not being able to watch a favorite video. To them it's a big, upsetting deal. But because you're a little older and more mature, you know that it's nothing to cry over, even while you understand that it's a big deal to them. Well, your parents are the same way. They can understand what you're saying, but they aren't going to have the same reaction as you. And that's okay. Remember, your parents' main concern is keeping you safe and healthy—sometimes you may think they're overreacting to something you're saying, but, again, they're just looking at things from a different point of view. The best thing to do during this roller coaster ride of emotional ups and downs is to keep the lines of communication open. It may be tough to talk things out. But it's always worth it.

Can't Shake the Blues?

Little ups and downs are normal along the road to adulthood. (Heck, they're normal even after you reach adulthood!) But if you ever feel hopelessly depressed or that life isn't worth living, talk to an adult right away. Sometimes people have chemical imbalances that interfere with their normal emotions. Other times you may be holding issues deep inside that you need to talk about because they're making you feel desperately unhappy. Either way, a professional can help you feel better.

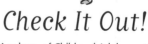

Check It Out!

American Academy of Child and Adolescent Psychiatry
3615 Wisconsin Avenue N.W.
Washington, D.C. 20016-3007
Phone: (202) 966-7300
Web site: www.aacap.org

American Psychological Association
750 First Street N.E.
Washington, D.C. 20002-4242
Phone: (800) 374-2721, (202) 336-5510
Web site: www.apa.org

Moods

Period

Welcome to "Womanhood!"

L ike the little dot of the same name that you put at the end of a sentence, your period is a punctuation mark in your life. It signals the end of girlhood and the grand entry into the big "W"—womanhood! Of course, you have plenty of maturing ahead of you before you can call yourself an adult. But once you start menstruating—the scientific term for your period—your body is able to have a baby, which is a big first step! Some girls get way excited about having their first period. Others are nervous or creeped out. All these emotions are completely natural and normal. The best way to be prepared for your first period, whether you're jumping for joy or quivering in your boots, is to be informed. Here are answers to questions girls most commonly ask.

"I wasn't really prepared to get my period,
so I wasn't sure what to expect.
Now that I have it, I still don't like it."

Chris, 13

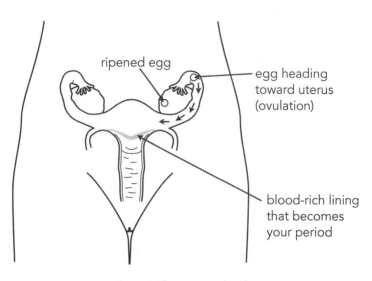

ripened egg

egg heading
toward uterus
(ovulation)

blood-rich lining
that becomes
your period

Figure 3. The menstrual cycle.

Q. What causes my period?

A. Your period is what happens when you're not pregnant. It happens in a monthly cycle as your body prepares to be pregnant. In a nutshell, it works like this (see figure 3):

Inside your body around your pelvis area you have two ovaries, almond-shaped organs that hold all your eggs (yep, just like fish and birds and a lot of other creatures, each egg is encased in a shell called a follicle. The ovaries are located near two little tunnels, called the Fallopian tubes, that lead into your uterus (also called the womb), the place where babies grow. Each month, a gland in your brain called the pituitary gland releases special hormones that cause an egg to ripen in your ovaries. When the egg is fully developed, another hormone is released that causes the egg to burst out of its follicle into the Fallopian tube and head toward your uterus. This event is *ovulation.* Meanwhile, the uterus, which is waiting for the egg, develops a thicker blood-rich lining so that if the egg becomes fertilized with sperm during this event, it can implant itself in this nourishing lining and grow into a baby. If the egg doesn't become fertilized, the uterus sheds the blood that made the uterus's lining thicker—this is the blood that comes out through your vagina that you know as your period. The next month, the process starts all over again: Another egg is released and the uterus grows a new lining.

Q. When will I get my first period?

A. No one can predict exactly when her first period will come. The most common age is about thirteen, but a girl can get her period anytime between her ninth and sixteenth birthdays. Though the exact day of its arrival is a mystery, you can often tell when you're getting close. If you've already sprouted pubic hair and other body hair, like under your arms, and your breasts have been developing, chances are your first period is right around the corner. You also can ask your mom or sisters when they got their first period. The timing of physical development often runs in the family.

Q. Can I tell when it's coming?

A. You can't really *feel* your period coming. But there are some telltale signs once you know what to look for. Some girls feel cramps in their lower abdomen (below your belly button). Some also have mood swings, feeling happy and giggly one moment and down in the dumps the next. (See PMS, page 128.) But until you've had a few periods, it's tough to pick up on these signs.

"Almost all my friends have gotten their periods, but I haven't yet. That feels a little weird to me."

Liz, 13

Q. What if I get it in school?

A. No worries! Everyone has heard the horror stories of the girl who was wearing white pants and got her period in the cafeteria while the whole world stared. But these are usually just

Period

that—stories. What's more likely to happen is you'll find a little blood on the toilet paper after you're done peeing. Or you'll see a few drops in your underwear. If your period pays you a surprise visit at school, don't freak. Many bathrooms have vending machines that sell tampons and pads. And the school nurse will almost definitely have a stash to help unsuspecting students. You also can make an "emergency pad" by rolling up some toilet paper and covering the crotch of your undies with it.

Q. Can I stop my period from coming?

A. Only by getting pregnant, which is definitely not an option you want right now! There are new birth control pills that stop your period from coming every month, but they don't stop it permanently. You just have it every four months instead. Some girls who are very, very active in sports stop having their periods, but this isn't considered healthy, so if this happens to you, definitely tell your mom so she can make an appointment for you to see a gynecologist.

Q. How long does a normal period last?

A. Usually between three and seven days. The flow of blood is not the same each day, however. Some days it may be no more than a trickle while other days it can feel like a gusher. Also, it's not uncommon to have some "spotting" (very light bleeding) in between your periods.

Q. Once it starts, will I have it at the same time every month?

A. Maybe, maybe not. When you first start menstruating, it may take a few months for your body to settle into a regular cycle. And even then, many women find that they never get their periods like clockwork. A normal cycle can last anywhere from nineteen to thirty-five days, with twenty-eight days being the average. Your cycle is measured from the first day of your current period to the first day of your next period. A lot of stuff can affect the length of your cycle, including traveling, stress, and being sick. Even living with other women can mess with

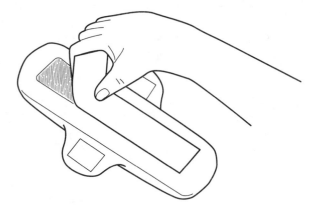

Figure 4. Sanitary pad.

your menstrual cycle. Women who spend a lot of time together sometimes start menstruating at the same time!

Q. How much will I bleed?

A. It seems like it's a lot, but most girls really only bleed a few teaspoons a day, or about a quarter cup for the entire cycle. And it's not a constant flow like a running faucet. Rather, it stops and starts throughout your period. While it's not unusual to have some heavy bleeding, if you totally soak through a pad or tampon every hour for a day or more, you should tell your parents and get checked by a doctor, just to be sure nothing's wrong.

Q. Which is better, pads or tampons?

A. It's a personal choice. There's good stuff and not-so-good stuff about both. Here's the scoop:

- **Pads.** Sanitary pads are external protection, meaning you just rip the backing off the adhesive strip and stick the pad onto your underwear (see figure 4). Available in all shapes and sizes, they're designed to pull blood away from you and into the pad. There's no risk of vaginal irritation or infection with pads. And they're super-easy to use. The downside? They feel kind of weird at first, like you're walk-

Period

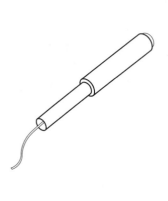

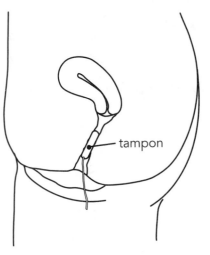

tampon

Figure 5. Tampon.

Figure 6. Tampon positioned inside the vagina.

ing around with a folded up washcloth between your legs. (But no one can see that you're wearing one, no matter how obvious you think it might be.) Also, you definitely know they're there when you're running and playing sports. And you have to change them every few hours or they can develop an odor. Never flush a pad down the toilet—it'll totally clog the plumbing. Instead, wrap it in some tissue paper and toss it in the trash or in the special containers that are in the stalls of many girls' bathrooms.

- **Tampons.** Tampons are internal protection. Made of compressed rolls of cotton with a string attached at one end, you insert them using a cardboard or plastic applicator (see figure 5). The tampon sits in your vagina where it absorbs blood before it has a chance to flow out. The string hangs outside your body, so you can pull it out when you need to change it (see figure 6), which is every four to eight hours. They come in different levels of absorbency, from junior or "lites" for very light flows to regular for medium flows to super-plus for heavy days. (To avoid complications, you should always choose the lowest absorbency you need.) Tampons are super comfortable and when you insert them correctly, you won't even know they're there. You can wear tampons while you're swimming. The downside? There's a very small risk of developing a condition called toxic shock syndrome (TSS). (See What You Need to Know About Toxic Shock Syndrome on page 127.) There's also a small learning curve with tampons—it can take a few tries to become comfortable inserting them. You can flush tampons, but usually not the applicators (unless the package says "flushable"). These tips can help with your first insertion:

- **Choose** junior or slender tampons—they're slimmer and easier to insert.

- **Relax.** It's natural to feel nervous when you're doing anything for the first time (especially inserting something into your body!), but your vaginal muscles tighten when you get nervous, which makes it much more difficult to insert a tampon successfully. So take a deep breath and relax.

- **Read** the instructions that come in the box with the tampons. They take you through the process step-by-step.

- **Lubricate** the tip of the applicator with a little K-Y Jelly (a special lube you can buy at the drugstore that is safe for vaginal use). It'll make it smoother to insert, especially when your vagina is dry.

The first few attempts can be tricky, for sure. But with a little practice and patience, inserting a tampon will eventually become as simple as putting on your shoes. Here's how it's done (remember to wash your hands before and after inserting a tampon):

1. Unwrap the tampon. Grip it around the large outer tube with your thumb and middle finger so that the fat part of

Period

Figure 7. Holding the tampon
for insertion.

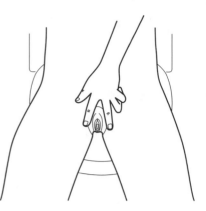
Figure 8. Opening the vagina
to insert a tampon.

the tampon is pointing toward your body and the skinny
tube of the tampon is pointed away from you (see figure 7).

2. Sit on the toilet with your legs open. Use your free hand to
   gently spread the lips of your vulva apart and expose the
   opening of your vagina (see figure 8).

3. Be sure you're holding the outer tube of the tampon along
   the ridges (where the outer tube and inner tube meet).
   Place the tip of the tampon into the opening of your
   vagina, pointing it up and angled toward your back (see
   figure 9). Relax and gently push the outer tube into your
   vagina until your thumb and middle finger are touching
   the vagina opening (see figure 10).

4. Now take your index finger, place it at the end of the
   skinny tube, and press it into the outer tube (see figure
   11). This inserts the tampon into your vagina where you
   won't feel it and it will absorb menstrual blood.

5. Gently pull the applicator tubes to remove them from
   your vagina (see figure 12) and throw them away. Remember you shouldn't feel a tampon once it's in. If you

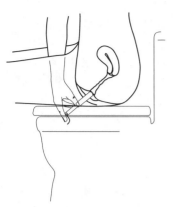

Figure 9. Beginning the
tampon insertion.

Figure 10. Completing the
tampon insertion.

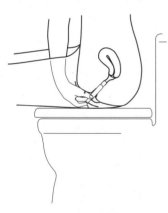

Figure 11. Depositing the
inside of the tampon.

Figure 12. Removing the applicator.

can feel it, it's not far enough into your body. Pull it out
(using the string) and try again with another one.

6. Once it's in place, the string should hang out of your
   vagina. When it's time to remove the tampon, simply sit
   back onto the toilet, relax, and gently pull the string. Flush
   the tampon down the toilet.

If you follow all the directions and still have trouble, there may be a physical reason. Some girls have an extra piece of skin located at the opening of the vagina called the hymenal strand, or more commonly, the hymen. This can make it difficult and sometimes painful to insert a tampon. Sometimes a girl manages to insert the tampon past the hymenal strand on one side or the other, only to find she can't get it out! The best thing to do if you are having lots of trouble getting a tampon in or out is to see a medical professional and ask for her help. If you do force a tampon in or out through your hymenal strand, you may feel a sharp pain and a see a few drops of bright red blood. That simply means you tore the hymenal strand, which is not harmful and should actually make it easier to get a tampon in next time.

"The worst thing about being a girl
is having your period. It is just gross."

Ashlyn, 13

Q. Does getting my period hurt? What can I do if it does?

A. Your period itself does not hurt. But the events that lead up to it can be uncomfortable and sometimes painful. To squeeze out the unneeded lining, the uterus muscles contract. These are the same muscles that help push a baby out when you're pregnant, so you know they've got some serious power! Though it sure doesn't hurt like labor, having your period also causes muscle contractions, or what we call menstrual cramps. A lot of things, from a warm bath to an over-the-counter pain reliever, can help. (See PMS, page 128 for more info.)

Q. Sometimes my period looks brown, not red—is this normal?

A. Yep. Menstrual blood may look bright red, brownish, or pinkish. All are normal.

Q. When I wake up and pee, I see blood clumps in the toilet. Am I okay?

A. You're A-okay. Thick clumps or clots are very common. Girls notice them especially in the morning, because you've been lying down and the blood has been building up and thickening in there. When you stand up, it flows out.

Q. If I don't get my period, does that mean I'm pregnant?

A. Maybe. If you've had unprotected intercourse—which is dangerous and definitely not smart—it's a possibility. If you have made a big mistake and had sex without protection, and you think you could be pregnant, you need to talk to your mom or dad pronto so they can help you get through this.

If you have not been sexually active, but still don't have your period, something else might be up. Some girls are irregular, especially when they first start menstruating, so it may be nothing at all. But if you miss two in a row, it's a good idea to see your doctor.

Also, don't think you can't get pregnant when you have your period. That's a common myth that has led to more than a few unwanted pregnancies. It's not common, but it's *not* impossible.

Q. Will I get periods forever?

A. Sometimes it may feel that way, but no, you won't. Just as the flow of hormones started your period, the slowdown of hormones that happens later in your adult life will bring it to a halt. This stoppage of your periods is called menopause, and it usually happens sometime around the age of fifty. Don't wish away your periods, by the way. They definitely can be a pain sometimes, but they're a sign that you're a healthy young woman who can someday give birth to some beautiful babies.

Q. Can I swim when I have my period?

A. Absolutely! But you should wear tampons, not pads, for protection. Pads would get pretty water-logged and probably wouldn't stay stuck to your swimming suit!

Period

Q. Will exercise make my period worse?

A. Quite the opposite! If you feel a little irritable and sluggish, exercise could be the best thing to lift your mood and make you feel better. You also can play sports during your period. Remember, professional women athletes and Olympic medal winners all get their periods, too, and that doesn't stop them from doing what they love and excelling at it.

No Period . . . Period?!?

There are complications that can be related to your period (or the lack of it). Keep an eye out for these.

It's not uncommon to get your period a little later than your friends, but if you're sixteen and you still haven't gotten your first period (or if you're fourteen and haven't had your first period or developed any other signs of puberty, like breasts and body hair), check with your doctor to be sure all those hormones are flowing properly and development is on the way.

Check It Out!

American College of Obstetrics and Gynecology (ACOG)
409 12th Street, S.W.
Washington, D.C. 20090-6920
Phone: (202) 638-5577
Web site: www.acog.com

Period

What You Need to Know
About Toxic Shock Syndrome

Toxic Shock Syndrome (TSS) is a rare, but potentially very serious disease that has occurred in some women using tampons. Though the risk of getting TSS is very low, it can be fatal on rare occasions, so it's important to take any symptoms seriously. If you have any of the following symptoms and are wearing a tampon, remove the tampon immediately, tell your parents to call a doctor, and make sure the doctor knows that you suspect that it could be TSS because TSS becomes a serious condition very quickly.

The warning signs are:

- Sudden high fever (102 or higher)

- Throwing up

- Diarrhea

- A sunburnlike rash

- Dizziness

- Fainting or almost fainting when you stand up

- Muscle aches

TSS has occurred more often in women using high-absorbency tampons, which is why it's important to always wear a tampon with the lowest absorbency for your flow.

Period

PMS

Decoding the Mysterious Period Before Your Period

Years ago, premenstrual syndrome (PMS) was considered a figment of women's imaginations. The belly bloating, cramps, mood swings, and pimples were all in our heads, doctors said. Then, once they finally admitted PMS actually *did* exist, they called it a "psychiatric disorder." Not much of an improvement, and many women didn't appreciate the implication that they were mentally unstable once a month! Today, medical professionals recognize that PMS is a biological condition, meaning that the causes are in your body, *not* your mind. Here are some things we know about this puzzling condition.

"Most of the puberty changes bug me, like having your period and stuff because of the pain. But I also think it's kind of neat that I'm becoming an adult."

Tara, 13

Q. What is PMS?

A. PMS is a group of physical and emotional symptoms that show up a few days to a couple of weeks before your period then disappear as soon as your period begins. Though it sounds like a disease, it's not. It's just a natural part of some girls' and women's menstrual cycle. Some girls don't have PMS at all. Some have just slight symptoms. Others can feel like a totally different person when they have PMS. How do you know if you have it? Keep track of your periods, and write about your experiences in a journal for a few months, making note of how you feel and what your moods are in the weeks approaching your period. If you notice that some symptoms show up pretty consistently, you probably experience PMS. Here are some of the symptoms to watch for:

- **Physical.** Bloating occurs, especially around your tummy; you have swollen or tender breasts, food cravings, pimple breakouts, cramps in your lower back or abdomen, overall puffiness, fatigue, headaches, and constipation (difficult bowel movements).

- **Emotional.** You experience grouchiness, have an unusually short temper, feel anger, sadness or depression, anxiety or tension, mental fatigue, and absentmindedness.

You probably won't have *all* these symptoms. But if you notice that you have a handful pretty regularly around your period, it's likely that you experience PMS.

Q. What causes PMS?

A. Believe it or not, we still don't entirely know. One of the culprits is definitely hormones. As your period approaches, your hormones shift dramatically, which can cause lots of physical and emotional symptoms. The cramping is mostly from the muscles in your uterus working to shed its old lining. And some experts think that some symptoms may even be caused or worsened by a lack of certain vitamins or minerals.

> "I don't understand why girls have
> to go through all this and boys don't."

Ashlyn, 13

Q. Will I have PMS every time I get my period?

A. Not necessarily. As your body changes, so can the way you experience your period. You may have your worst cramping and mood swings now and few problems later. Or you may have almost no symptoms now, only to have headaches and bloating pop up when you're older. Your symptoms can stay much the same from period to period. Or they can change from one month to the next. A lot also depends on what's going on in your life at the time—stuff like diet, exercise, and stress can all affect how PMS affects you.

Q. Can I do anything to make my PMS better?

A. You bet! Here are some "home remedies" to help you beat the worst of PMS:

- **Eat the good stuff.** You may crave chocolate and potato chips, but too much sugar and salt can contribute to your mood swings and bloating. The better choice is to munch on healthful foods like fruits, vegetables, whole grains, and lean protein foods like fish. Trade in sugary, caffeine-filled soda for lowfat milk or water. You certainly shouldn't be drinking alcohol yet, but it's a good idea to limit it when you *are* old enough to drink because it can worsen PMS symptoms.

- **Move your body.** Exercise is a big-time PMS reliever. Rollerblading, riding your bike, or just taking a long walk can ease cramps, reduce water retention (which causes bloating), and chase away the blues. You may not feel like moving at first, but once you get going, you're bound to feel better.

- **Chill out!** Stress totally makes PMS worse. Learning to relax is important at any time of life, but especially when your hormones have your nerves on edge. Try taking some quiet time in your room to listen to music and write in your journal. Learn to practice yoga, deep breathing, or simple meditation. Avoid situations and people that stress you out if you can.

- **Take a soak.** A warm, bubbly bath can be just what the doctor ordered to soothe a crampy back and tummy. Plus it relaxes you, too, for a doubly good benefit!

- **Try over-the-counter pain relief.** Sometimes all the relaxation and fresh air in the world won't ease your headache or calm your cramps. If pain's got you down and you need relief to function, it's time to give some over-the-counter pain relievers a try. Simple medications like ibuprofen can provide some much-needed relief. Your mom or doctor can help you choose a brand that is safe and effective.

Q. *Is there anything good about PMS?*

A. When you read all those possible symptoms, PMS sounds awful for sure! But surprisingly, it's not such a bad time for many girls and women. Some say they have increased energy, expressive dreams, and more focus during this time of month. And even if you have some unpleasant symptoms, like cramping or a short temper, it's not necessarily a bad thing. It's just your body's way of telling you that your period is on its way. Some women even enjoy the moodiness, because it gives them a chance to reflect on life and makes them less willing to put up with people who annoy them! The trick is learning how your body responds during your cycle, then enjoying the positive aspects of being a growing young woman and finding the healthiest, most effective way of handling symptoms that make you uncomfortable.

Don't Let PMS Run Your Life!

Some physical discomfort and emotional lows are completely normal during the days or weeks before your period. But if the physical pain or the mood swings become unbearable, don't write it off as a girl thing you have to live with. Though it's not common, some girls and women can experience PMS symptoms so severe that it's almost impossible to do even simple daily tasks at school or work. If that's how it is with you, your doctor can refer you to a PMS specialist who can use various treatments to make your premenstrual life livable again.

Check It Out!

American College of Obstetrics and Gynecology (ACOG)
409 12th Street, S.W.
Washington, D.C. 20090-6920
Phone: (202) 638-5577
Web site: www.acog.com

Sexuality

The Good, the Bad, and the Totally Confusing!

Nothing about puberty is as exciting, distracting, or confusing as the development of sexual feelings. As your body prepares you to be able to get pregnant and nourish babies (through your period and breast development), it's perfectly natural to start developing romantic or sexual feelings. You may notice boys more than you used to or spend time conjuring up romantic fantasies about your favorite singer. Sexual feelings may be strong and can be fun and scary all at the same time. But like everything else that happens in puberty, the more you understand these feelings, the easier they'll be to handle. Here's what you need to know.

Q. Sometimes I just look at a cute boy in class and I have strange feelings "down there." What's going on?

A. Hormones! As you produce more gender- and sex-related hormones like estrogen and testosterone, you develop a natural "sex drive," which means you become more sensitive to sexual stuff around you—including cute boys. When you see something—a cute guy in science class or even just a poster of a sexy celebrity—you find attractive, that information is sent from your eyes to your brain, which processes the information and tells your body how to respond—in this case by getting sexually aroused or "turned on." When you get aroused your body sends more blood to your genitals (called engorgement), so you feel some tension down there. Your body also produces fluids that lubricate your vagina, so you also may feel damp or wet. Arousal doesn't just affect your genitals; it affects your whole body. You may notice that your heart beats faster, your skin becomes flushed and sensitive to the touch, and your nipples may become swelled and erect as well. The funniest part about all this is that you don't even have to *see* a cute boy to bring on this cascade of physical changes. Just *thinking* about something sexy can make you feel aroused. These feelings can be strong and seemingly come out of nowhere, but they also pass almost as quickly—especially if you're in school and need to get your mind on your class work!

Q. My friends and I talk about sex a lot. Sometimes I feel guilty afterward. Is talking about sex bad?

A. Talking about sex isn't bad unless you're saying hurtful things about someone. Otherwise, it is *very* normal and common for girls to think, talk about, be interested in, and giggle over sexual topics. It's also normal to feel a little guilty. Though our society seems obsessed with sex, we frequently get the message that sex is "dirty" or "bad," so we feel a little guilty for thinking about it. And since sexual feelings are very personal, we also can feel embarrassed when we talk about sex. Just remember that sex is a perfectly normal part of who you are. Without sexual thoughts and feelings, none of us would be here. So try not to feel too bad. One word of caution about talking about sex with your friends: Misinformation! Sometimes girls think they know everything about guys and sex, when they really don't. That's how myths and bad information get passed along. When talking with your girlfriends about sex, try to keep the facts straight. Use books like this one and other factual resources to answer your questions about stuff like sexual arousal and getting pregnant. The more facts you have, the better choices you'll be able to make about sex as you get older.

Q. I know boys masturbate. Do girls?

A. You bet. Guys tend to talk about it more (big surprise) than girls do, but girls also masturbate. Masturbation is touching or rubbing your genitals, particularly the vulva and clitoris in girls, for sexual pleasure. If you continue masturbating long enough, you may have what is known as an *orgasm*. Though it's pretty tough to describe, an orgasm is basically the release of all the sexual tension you build up when you're aroused. It's usually a pleasant rush of warm, pulsing muscle contractions from your genital region. Some people masturbate a lot; some only once in a while. Some people never masturbate, though most people try it at some point in their lives. Even very little children occasionally touch themselves because they're curious and find that it feels good. Some people worry about masturbating "too much." Unless you're masturbating so much that it's keeping you from normal activity, like playing with friends and doing your homework, you shouldn't worry. Also, you've probably heard all the stories about masturbation making you blind or putting hair on your palms. None of those crazy stories are true. On the contrary, masturbation can be quite healthy. It gives you a safe outlet for your sexual feelings and lets you get to know your body and your sexual self better.

That said, although masturbation is not unhealthy, there are some people and certain religious groups who believe that people should not masturbate. That is a decision you will eventually have to make for yourself. If you believe masturbation is wrong, it's perfectly acceptable and normal to decide not to do it.

Q. Does kissing count as sex?

A. Yes and no. Kissing is *not* the same as sexual intercourse—where a man inserts his penis into a woman's vagina. But it is a sexual activity. It can lead to other sexual activity, or you can just kiss and not go any further. Kissing is usually the first sexual activity girls have. You almost always remember your first kiss.

> "In fifth grade, we had the 'sex talk' class, but we really didn't learn very much about it and haven't gotten any more information, though I'm in seventh grade now. I learn most of that stuff from my mom."

Ashlyn, 13

Q. There's a boy I like, but I'm not ready for sex. What should I do?

A. Whoa! Slow down. Just because you like a boy doesn't mean it will immediately lead to sex. Even when you're older and dating, you certainly shouldn't expect that you'll have a sexual relationship with every boy you go out with. Though television shows and movies make it seem like guys and girls can't do anything without having their hands all over each other, you *can* spend time with someone and be close with them without so much as kissing or holding hands with them. Also, "sex" includes a whole spectrum of activities, including kissing; hugging; touching each other in sexual and nonsexual places; and, finally, if and when you're ready, sexual intercourse. You're totally in charge of how far you go with any boy, and you have years and years ahead of you to get involved at any sexual level, so you absolutely should not feel rushed or pressured to do anything you're not ready for. Remember—sex isn't just physical. It's also a powerful emotional activity. Though your body may feel "aroused" and "ready" for the physical activity, most girls don't feel ready for the emotional impact of sexual activity until they are older. So for now, go ahead and enjoy your crushes and spend time with boys at dances and sports events, but don't feel that you need to jump into sex of any kind.

Q. How do you know when you're ready for sex?

A. A *lot* of factors go into making that decision! You have to consider your own beliefs, your parent's beliefs, your religion's beliefs, and your personal values and morals. You may feel it's right to wait for marriage to have a sexual relationship. Or you may think kissing or other activity is okay when you're a little older and really care about someone. No matter what, you definitely need to consider your own feelings about the relationship. You need to know someone really well to consider any sexual activity with them. Do you really care about this person? Do you really trust them? Is this something you really want to do, or are you just doing it because you're curious or feel it's the grown-up thing to do? Finally, whatever you do, don't ever let someone pressure you into having any sexual activity you're not ready for or don't want to do. Don't fall for come-ons like "If you loved me, you would . . . ." The answer to that is always "If you loved me, you wouldn't pressure me." Don't worry about hurting anyone's feelings. Anyone who really cares about you will understand. And if they don't really care about you, they don't deserve your affection. Respect yourself and have confidence that you know what's right for you and your body. You need to take care of yourself first and foremost.

Q. My friends are boy crazy, but I'm just not interested yet. What's wrong with me?

A. Absolutely nothing! Just like you grow taller and develop breasts at a different rate than your friends, you also develop sexual interests at different rates. And even when you're older, you may find that boys or men aren't as huge of a deal to you as they seem to be to other folks. No worries. Your romantic feelings are all just part of who you are. So don't worry about not being boy crazy. You have a lot of years ahead of you for sexual feelings. Take the time right now to explore all your other interests, whether music, sports, school, community service, or whatever. That makes you a more well-rounded person than just obsessing about boys 24/7 anyway!

Q. What is homosexuality?

A. Homosexuality (*homo* literally means "same") means having sexual feelings or performing sexual activity with someone of the same sex. However, having sexual thoughts or experiences with someone of your same gender does not necessarily mean you're "gay" or homosexual. Many people have sexual thoughts about someone (real or imaginary) of the same sex at some point in their lives. Most people don't consider themselves to be gay or lesbian (another term for homosexual women) unless their primary sexual thoughts and experiences involve the same sex. You've likely heard people make cruel or insulting remarks about homosexuality. There are some people who feel homosexuality is wrong or sinful. Many others feel it is a normal and acceptable way to be. Whatever your beliefs, homosexuality is fairly common, and it's not a reason to be mean to someone.

Q. My parents always say I can talk to them about anything, but won't they get mad if I bring up sex?

A. They may be a little embarrassed—just like you are—but chances are they won't get mad. In fact, they may actually feel *relieved* that you're bringing it up! Most parents want to talk to their kids about sex, but they often don't know how to get the conversation started. Girls who talk to their parents about sex usually end up much better informed than those who don't. Your parents are also more apt to trust your judgment if you come to them with your questions about sexuality. If they *do* get upset that you're bringing up these subjects or if they say you're too young, try telling them that you're just hearing a lot of stuff at school and you want to know the real facts—that's why you're asking them.

Q. Can you get pregnant if you don't "go all the way?"

A. Yes. Sperm are awesome swimmers. So even if a tiny drop of semen (the substance that comes from a man's penis when he ejaculates) gets on the outside of your vagina, it's possible for a sperm to swim into your body and fertilize an egg. Whenever you decide to engage in any sexual activity where an exposed penis and vagina are involved, it's important to be extremely careful and use protection, like a condom (a barrier that goes over the penis). And it's not just pregnancy you have to worry about, but sexually transmitted diseases as well. Yet another reason to take your time with sexual activity and to be totally informed before you do anything.

Q. My mom is always warning me about "diseases" people can get from having sex. Can you get a disease even your first time?

A. It sounds hard to believe, but, yes, you can. In fact, you can get a disease from a boy even if *he* has never had sex before because he may have picked up a disease from something else—like using drugs. According to a recent survey, the rate of HIV infection (getting the virus that causes AIDS) in girls aged fifteen to nineteen went up *117 percent* during the mid-1990s. That's a huge jump. It's very, very important for girls who become sexually active in their teens to use protection like condoms. Even better: Wait to have sex until you're older and in a committed relationship with someone you know, trust, and love. It's safer physically and emotionally.

Sexuality

Don't Tolerate the Wrong Kind of Touch!

Remember, your body is yours and yours alone. You don't have to share it with anyone. In fact, it's a crime for someone to touch you sexually when you don't want them to. If anyone—a stranger, a boy you know, or even a family member—touches you in a sexual way against your will, tell a trusted adult immediately. Girls often feel guilty or ashamed when someone sexually violates them. But remember: *It's never your fault.* You have nothing to feel guilty or ashamed about. You're the one who was molested. It may be tempting to pretend it never happened and hope it doesn't happen again, but to protect yourself and maybe other girls from the same abuse, it's important that you tell someone.

Check It Out!

SIECUS (Sexuality Information and Education Council of the United States)
Main Office
130 West 42nd Street,
Suite 350
New York, New York 10036-7802
Phone: (212) 819-9770
Web site: www.siecus.org

Web site: www.askdoctormarla.com (an online resource of information on relationships, sexuality, and more; hosted by a family practitioner and adolescent medicine specialist with thirteen years experience working with preteens and teens and the special issues they face growing up)

Sexuality

Stress

Chill Out!

O kay, here's the catch: Growing up is cool because it means more freedom, more challenges, and more opportunities. Growing up also means more responsibilities, more pressures, and, ultimately, more stress—and that's anything but cool. Stress is that nerve-jangling, butterflies-in-stomach, anxious feeling you get when you're feeling overwhelmed. Tons of things can cause stress, and it's different for everyone. For some girls, schoolwork causes stress. For others, it's tough times at home. For many more, it's a combination of everything rolled up into one big stress bomb that makes you feel ready to explode. The bad news is, stress doesn't go away. In fact, it often increases with college, new jobs, marriage, and all that other adult stuff. The good news is, you *can* totally learn how to handle stress and, in some cases, even get rid of some of it. Here are some soothing answers to questions girls commonly have about stress.

"When something bothers me, I try to walk away and take deep breaths so I don't get mad over something silly!"

Britany, 11

Q. Can stress make you sick?

A. You bet! Stress not only makes you feel sick—the upset stomach and achy head—but unless you do something to tame it, stress can lower your immunity so you're more vulnerable to stuff like colds and viruses. That's why it's better to beat your stress than to let it beat you up!

Q. My parents say I have it so much easier than they did, but it doesn't feel that way! Is it harder to be a kid today?

A. In some ways, yes; in some ways, no. Your parents say it's easier because kids today have so many resources at their fingertips. More families have more money, so you can have more of the things you want. More kids can go to college than ever before. Kids, especially girls, have many more school, sports, and career choices than they've ever had. More kids have access to computers, cell phones, and all kinds of media than ever before, too. The funny thing is that all these choices and opportunities are exactly what can make life tougher for kids today than it was in the past. When girls didn't have many choices growing up, it was easy for them to feel terrific and successful. Now that people finally realize that girls can be great at a lot of things, you know you can aspire to almost anything you want, so it's tougher to decide what you really want to do and to try to do your best at everything. Also, kids become more involved in activities like sports and clubs at earlier ages than in the past. And while it's fun and exciting, it also means a lot of practicing, and scheduling, and, yes, stress. Finally, let's face it, life is more complicated. More parents are divorced, families move more because of job changes, and sometimes it can feel like there isn't enough time to just hang out and be a kid.

All that said, your parents probably had stresses that you never dream of, like having to work to help support their family or never being able to afford new clothes. So you shouldn't walk around feeling all "woe is me" either. Everyone grows up with stress; it's just different from generation to generation.

> "My parents fight a lot.
> It's very stressful to be in our house."

Julie, 11

Q. I get so nervous before tests, I feel like throwing up. How can I calm down?

A. Take a deep breath! You are not alone. According to "Teens Before Their Time" research from the Girl Scouts, tests come up again and again as "the worst part of school" among eight- to twelve-year-old girls surveyed. Many girls get so worked up over tests that they cry, feel tired and unhappy, or just dread going to school. The thing to remember is that tests are not the end of the world, no matter how much they may feel like it. Even if you don't totally shine in a particular subject, that doesn't mean you won't have a bright future! The other thing about tests is that you can bring your stress about them way down by studying. Think about it. You worry about tests because you want to do well. If you stay on top of your class work, study (and that doesn't mean try to cram it all in the night before!), and do your homework, chances are you'll feel confident that you know the subject. When you feel confident, you feel a whole lot less stress. Also, realize that *everyone* gets nervous before tests. It's perfectly natural. Just remember the last time you were really nervous about an exam and you ended up doing well. Keep focused on the positive.

Q. Sometimes I feel so overwhelmed by all the stuff I have to do that I don't want to do anything. What's wrong with me?

A. Nothing's wrong with you. It's normal to feel overwhelmed when you have tons to do. Truth is, everyone needs a little chill time, when they just hang out and do nothing at all. The trick is finding a balance. If you feel overwhelmed all the time, maybe you really *do* have too much on your plate. Take a look

Stress

at all the activities you do. If you're in sports, dance lessons, cheerleading, and youth group, it's little wonder you would feel like stress is suffocating you! Pick only the activities you really, really love, making sure that you leave some free time to kick back, relax, and daydream.

Q. I find everything stressful! Help!

A. If everything in your life is stressful, you need to find some things to do that are nothing but enjoyable. Most of the time the stuff that we find stressful—school and sports—are stressful because they're based on our performance. We get nervous because we're afraid we won't do well. We compare ourselves to others, and we're afraid we don't measure up. So instead, find a hobby or activity that isn't based on performance or success. Try writing poetry, Rollerblading through a park, painting, or doing some kind of craft like pottery or jewelry making. When you do stuff just for the love of doing it, there's nothing to feel stressed about.

Practicing some sort of relaxation exercise every day can also help you beat and prevent stress. Give one of these a try:

- **Deep breathing.** A quick destressor you can do absolutely everywhere—even in class right before that big test—is deep breathing. Simply inhale sl-o-o-wly, nice and deep. Hold your breath a second or two, then sl-o-o-wly let it all out. Do this a couple times and you'll feel less stressed for sure. And it's not like you have to make loud whooshing sounds when you do this. You can do it quietly through your nose, and no one will know you're destressing.

- **Exercise.** Running, riding a bike, swimming, and just moving your body is a great way to beat stress. When you exercise, you burn off all the yucky stress hormones that your body produces when you're stressed out. Try to have some playtime every day.

- **Visualization.** Sit in your room, close your eyes, take deep breaths, and pretend you're on the beach, on the top of a mountain, or in some other peaceful, quiet, relaxing place. Feel yourself calm down as you imagine how this magical place looks, smells, and feels.

- **Baths.** Pour yourself a toasty, bubble-filled bath and feel the stress slip away.

- **Books.** Losing yourself in a great book is a huge tension tamer. It's even better when you're snuggled under the covers in bed.

- **Music.** It's tough to feel stressed out listening to your favorite song. A lot of girls blow off anxiety by kickin' it in their rooms and listening to their favorite tunes.

- **Progressive relaxation.** If you're feeling all bunched up with stress, progressive relaxation is a great way to unwind. Lie on your back and close your eyes. Then, starting at your toes, wiggle and relax each area of your body— your feet, your legs, your arms, all the way up to the top of your head.

Finally, remember sometimes we're the worst producers of our stress. Instead of coming home and staring at your pile of homework and worrying about it and stressing over it, try just sitting down and doing it. Once it's out of the way, you'll be stress free and free to play!

Stress

Share Some Stress!

Sometimes the stuff you're stressed about may be too big for you to deal with alone, no matter how many relaxation exercises you do. If your parents are getting a divorce, for instance, you may be carrying a big-time burden of stress that you can't seem to shake. Talk to someone. Sometimes working through your feelings with a counselor, favorite teacher, or trusted relative can help relieve stress and lift your spirits.

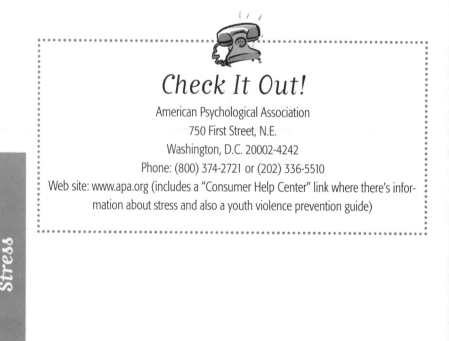

Check It Out!

American Psychological Association
750 First Street, N.E.
Washington, D.C. 20002-4242
Phone: (800) 374-2721 or (202) 336-5510
Web site: www.apa.org (includes a "Consumer Help Center" link where there's information about stress and also a youth violence prevention guide)

Stress

Well-Being

Staying Safe and Secure

Television shows and commercials often depict childhood as a carefree, idyllic time filled with nothing but sunny days and good times. That's a great way to sell soft drinks, but any kid growing up in today's world knows that while being a kid can be fun for sure, it can also be pretty scary. There's often violence in schools, upheaval at home, and let's not even mention all the stuff that goes on in the world! The good news is that even though bad stuff does happen, there's usually more to be happy about than to be sad about. And with the right support system and mindset, this time in your life can truly be one of the best. Here are some tips.

"Everyone wants to be better: To have better grades, better clothes, a better car, more money, to be more glamorous. The list goes on. I believe perfection can never be achieved because we constantly want more.
Where does it stop? Many negative things can happen to your mind when searching for perfection."

Melissa, 13

Q. I get so scared when I read the newspaper and watch television that sometimes I don't want to grow up and go out on my own.

A. That's a completely understandable reaction to all the terrible stuff newspapers and television news programs show us. Even adults feel that way sometimes! But what adults know—and what can help you feel safer in a sometimes unsafe world—is that the media show you every horrible thing that happens everywhere on the planet. When someone hurts people in Africa, you can read about it in Idaho the next day. What you need to remember is that there are *billions* of people on the planet, *millions and millions* right here in the United States. So, those ten or fifteen bad things you see or hear in the news are very, very small compared to all the good things that are happening in countless other places around the country and the world. Also, while it's a good idea to keep up with current events by reading the paper and watching the news, you can definitely get too much news. It might be just as good an idea to limit your exposure to news media, maybe to, say, a few minutes a day.

Also, pay close attention to all the safety advice you get at school and home. It may sound like lecturing, but when your teachers and parents talk to you about being cautious of strangers, buddying up whenever you go somewhere, learning escape routes, and avoiding dangerous situations, they are simply trying to protect you from the bad stuff they know can happen. The best advice for staying safe and sound is to follow their advice. Remember, too, that you can always talk to your mom or dad if you're concerned about your safety. They have a lot of experience in the world and can help you feel better.

Q. There are some bullies in my school that pick on me and my friends. I hate going to school in the morning—what can I do?

A. Bullying is a problem that has been around as long as people who don't feel good about themselves have been around, because that's who the bullies are. Many adults faced bullies when they were young, and many kids face bullies today. Since bullies are usually people who feel bad about themselves, they pick on other people hoping to make them feel bad, too. This is how bullies feel better about themselves. But that doesn't mean you have to take it. Bullies want a reaction, so do your best not to let them provoke you or make you mad or upset. Ignore bullies or stand up to them, letting them know that you're not going to fight and you're not going to let them ruin your day. Also, don't laugh when bullies make fun of someone else. When bullies lose their audience or fail to get the reaction they want, they'll move on. If the bullying doesn't stop, or gets worse, talk to someone—either your parents or a trusted teacher, and ask for their help. It's not tattling when you're trying to stop someone from hurting you and your friends. And chances are if these bullies are bothering you, they're bothering others, too. Your teachers will be able to take steps to make it stop.

"I've been having trouble in school.
My parents were really worried. But now some teachers are helping me find classes I'm really good at, so I feel better and am much happier."

Chris, 13

Q. I'm having a tough time in one of my classes this year. I'm so afraid of failing and ruining my life. How can I get through this?

A. Take a deep breath. Doing poorly in one class, whether it's math, geography, or English, will *not* ruin your life. In fact, even doing poorly in more than one class will not ruin your life. What you need is a little tutoring and a little perspective. First, talk to your parents about what's going on. They may be able to provide extra attention to help you with the subject you're having trouble with or even get you a tutor, a private instructor who can spend additional time with you and teach you the subject in a way that's easier for you to understand. Second, talk to your parents about your fear of failing a class and what it means for your life. When you're eleven or twelve, you don't have a lot of life experience. Maybe you never did poorly in something before. Or you always hear how important grades are for going to college and getting a good job. So it's natural to be scared. Your parents may very well tell you that they, too, had subjects they struggled with or times when they didn't succeed. But it didn't wreck their lives. They grew from those mistakes, and ultimately they learned what they do well and succeeded in those areas.

Nobody Deserves Abuse!

One of the things you need most for your well-being is a safe, secure home. Unfortunately, for some kids, home is the place they are least safe. If someone at home is hurting you, it can feel like the worst thing in the world—and the hardest to deal with. But it's important that you tell someone—a trusted teacher or other family member or maybe the parent of one of your friends—who can help you get out of your potentially dangerous and definitely unhealthy situation. You can also call the National Child Abuse Hotline: (800) 4-A-CHILD (422-4453). This hotline is open twenty-four hours a day to help children who are being abused. They can help you and whoever is hurting you.

Check It Out!

Safe Culture Project
802 North Lincoln
Creston, Iowa 50801
Phone: (800) 606-9750
Web site: www.safeculture.com

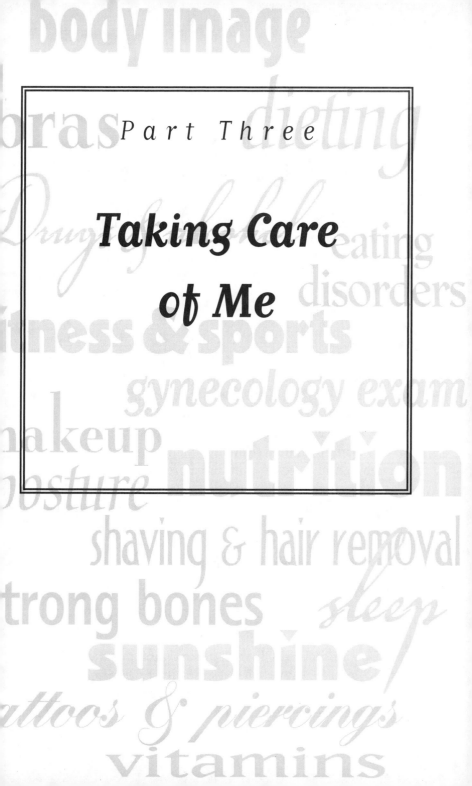

Part Three

Taking Care
of Me

Body Image

Get Real About Your Body!

For many girls the hardest part about being a girl is feeling comfortable with and in their bodies. Everywhere you look—MTV, *Teen* magazine, billboards, movies—there are superthin, seemingly perfect girls with "just-right" bodies, bright white smiles, and flawless skin. When girls take a peek in their own bedroom mirrors and see that the image looking back doesn't totally match the ones they see in magazines and on television, many start feeling bad about themselves. And as we see more and more media images, the problem can get worse. Studies show that more girls at younger ages are struggling with bad body image—and that's a drag! Fortunately, once you understand a little more about those bodies you see all over the media—as well as about your own—it's easier to feel good about your body and everything it can do.

Q. What's so bad about wanting to look like the girls in teen magazines? They're just real girls, right?

A. They are real girls. But that doesn't mean that they're "realistic" girls or that the pictures you see of them are really what they look like! First, you have to realize that we're all born with a certain body type. Some of us are curvy, with full breasts and

154

hips; some of us are less curvy and more angular, and others are broader and more muscular. We're born destined to be a certain height with legs that are a certain length and breasts that are a certain size. The models you see may have long legs, you may have shorter legs. And it's just a plain fact that they won't become long legs—it doesn't matter how much you wish or how hard you try. It's better to appreciate your own body—after all it's the only one you have!—for all of its special qualities. How fast can your legs run? How hard can you kick a ball? What great things can your body do for you?

"I love my body because I'm not fat and not skinny, so I think I'm perfect! But I think everyone at this age shouldn't worry about their body too much. Or about being fat!"

Britany, 11

Still dying to look like a "model" or your favorite celebrity? Consider this: When you see those girls and women in magazines, in movies, and on television, you're not seeing what they look like in real life. Before a photo shoot, before someone goes on television, before a scene is shot in a film, there is a *whole team of stylists* that spends hours putting on tons of makeup, covering every single pimple and blemish. Professionals fix her hair and use heavy-duty hair spray to cement it in place (sometimes she even has fake hair extensions put on). And then they plow through piles of clothes to find that one ideal outfit. Even then, the clothing is adjusted to look perfect. They pin it, tape it, and staple it, so it hangs a certain way and doesn't move. Occasionally, the model or actress may even have to alter her body by wearing a push up bra or even taping her boobs in place! They then take dozens and dozens of pictures or shoot lots and lots of film to find that one perfect shot. Finally—and this is the most important thing to understand—once the film or pictures are done, special technicians actually *alter the film to remove any imperfections!* That means they use an airbrush to shave down the hips and tummy from the photo. They also use special tools on a computer to smooth out her complexion, brighten her eyes, and whiten her smile. That's why trying to look like famous people is such a waste of time—not to mention damaging to your own self-esteem. *Nobody* could look like that—including the model herself.

Q. I feel chubby all over, I'm not happy about my body, but my mom says I can't diet. What can I do?

A. Dieting at this time of your life can be dangerous to your health (see Dieting, page 169). Plus, dieting is usually a bad idea even as you get older, past your teens and into your twenties and on. The dieting industry in this country is a multimillion-dollar business because diets don't work, yet people keep hoping the next one they try will. So they go from one fad diet scheme to the next, spending tons of money and continuing to be unhappy with their weight. The best approach to having a healthy weight is to eat a healthful diet with a lot of fruits and veggies and whole grains and to get out and play as often as you can.

About feeling chubby all over, it *is* possible that you have a little excess body weight—but it's probably very, very temporary! Remember, right now you're entering the biggest growth spurt of your life. That means you'll gain weight and grow taller. But those two things don't always happen *exactly* at the same time. So it's very common for girls to put on a little weight first, then shoot up like a weed. Be patient and let your body go through this amazing process of growing up. And remember: Most of us are more critical of ourselves than others are of us. So even if you have hit a brief chubby period, you probably notice more than anyone else.

Q. Boys like thin girls with big breasts. How will I ever find a boyfriend if I don't look the right way?

A. Look around you, girl! Shopping malls, movie theaters, and the downtown streets are loaded with girls and women who aren't thin and don't have big breasts, yet are in happy relationships with boys and men. Boys like all kinds of girls. In fact, studies show that when boys and girls are shown pictures of different female body types and asked to pick the one they think looks best, the boys almost always choose a stronger, fuller, more normal-looking body type than the girls, who get stuck thinking skinnier is better.

What's more, you don't need to go through life looking at your body the way you think boys, or any other people, see you! Look at your body through your own two eyes. What do you like about it? What makes your body special? What kinds of things—a steamy shower or a snuggly blanket—make your body feel good? Learning to see your body without imagining how other people see it can be tough. But once you do, you'll be more comfortable and confident.

Q. What if I really don't like my legs?

A. First, try to look at your body as a whole, not just a bunch of parts like legs, breasts, arms, hips. Girls sometimes get fixated on one particular body part, without appreciating how the rest of their body looks. Your legs probably fit just right with the rest of your body. Not to mention that your legs can do a lot of cool stuff like hike up mountains, race down fields, and jump high to shoot baskets. If you're still stuck feeling unhappy about your legs, try finding a feature on your body that you're really proud of. It can be anything from your arms to your eyes to your smile. Whenever you find yourself thinking bad thoughts about your legs, turn your attention to the stuff you like instead.

Q. Every time I go shopping, I come back feeling depressed with my body. How can I feel better?

A. A lot of clothing for girls—and women—is designed with just one body type in mind. There's no way that everyone will feel comfortable in a belly shirt or in low-slung board shorts. What's comfortable and flattering for one person is not always comfortable and flattering for another. The trick here is to find a style that works for you. Jeans come in all different cuts; skirts come in a lot of lengths; shirts can be long, short, tailored, or baggy. If one style doesn't look quite right when you're trying on clothes, pick something completely different. Also, try to find clothes that are functional for the activities you like to do. If you play sports, go for casual, sporty styles like warm-up pants and T-shirts; if you hike, look for outdoorsy clothes like natural fabrics in earthy tones. They don't just look great, but feel and perform great, too.

"I'm perfectly happy with my body.
I love wearing new clothes!"

Julie, 11

Q. Can I be happy with my body even in a bathing suit?

A. Yes, you can! But it'll take some practice. It's understandable you may feel a little "body anxious" about going to the pool or the beach because your body is pretty exposed. Here's an exercise to try next time you go to the beach. Sit down for five minutes and look at all the imperfect bodies you can find in swimsuits (there are a lot of them; you could probably spend fifteen minutes or more). Once you've done that, check out the ones who look completely confident and happy, playing and swimming and walking tall and proud. They're the ones to learn from! They know that it doesn't matter a bit if your hair's a little frizzy or your breasts are big or small. What matters is that you're on the beach, it's beautiful and fun, and you have a body that lets you enjoy it all.

Another way to feel good about your body more of the time: Take up a sport. Girls who are active and play sports feel more comfortable in their bodies no matter what they're wearing because they develop a healthy relationship with their bodies. They focus more on what their bodies can do—swim through water, pedal a bike, run, jump, kick—than constantly worrying about how they look. As a benefit, regular activity helps you maintain a strong, healthy body that glows and feels great.

Q. What can I do about all the stuff I see on television that makes me feel bad about myself?

A. For one, you can turn it off! A lot of experts believe that girls who watch more television are more likely to have bad body images and have problems with eating disorders. Whether you realize it or not, all those images you see, especially in videos and advertisements, affect the way you see yourself. Remember, the makers of those commercials are trying to sell you stuff—from soda to makeup to chewing gum—that they're promising will make you feel better, look better, and have more friends. They're *trying* to make you feel a little bad about yourself so you'll plunk down money and buy their product, which, by the way, *won't* make you look better, feel better, or have more friends. Don't fall for it, and don't waste hours and hours of your day watching TV. You have better things to do—like read, write poetry, play outside, or just hang out, listen to music, and daydream.

If you feel strongly enough, you can also take action! Most products have addresses on the label, so if that product has an advertisement that you think is bad for a girl's body image, write them a letter. Get your friends involved, too. If a company hears from enough unhappy people, it's likely that they'll change their tune.

Squash the Body Image "Bug!"

Bad body image can be contagious! If your friends spend a lot of time worrying if they're too fat or their hair looks good, chances are you will, too. Likewise, if you start freaking about your thighs, your friends will start worrying about theirs. Then everyone feels bad! Stop the spread of this bad-body-image disease by saying nice things about each other. For one full week make a pact with your pals that you won't dis anything about your bodies. You can even take it one step further and list all the positive things about each other—not just body and appearance stuff, but also things you do well and other positive qualities. See how much better you feel at the end of the week!

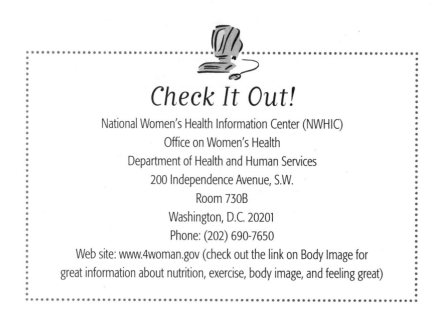

Check It Out!

National Women's Health Information Center (NWHIC)
Office on Women's Health
Department of Health and Human Services
200 Independence Avenue, S.W.
Room 730B
Washington, D.C. 20201
Phone: (202) 690-7650
Web site: www.4woman.gov (check out the link on Body Image for
great information about nutrition, exercise, body image, and feeling great)

Bras

When You Need Some Support

Once you develop breasts, the next step is deciding on a bra. Girls wear bras for several reasons. One, it's simply more comfortable to have your breasts supported while you walk and play, rather than having them jiggling around beneath your shirt. For girls with large breasts, a supportive bra may help keep breasts from sagging over time. Finally, it's more socially acceptable to wear a bra than to go braless. As you may already have noticed, breasts attract a lot of attention! Bouncing, braless breasts get even *more* attention—mostly unwanted! Eventually, most girls decide to take the plunge and buy a bra. Here's what you need to know when you decide it's bra time.

Q. How do I know if I need a bra?

A. There's no magical age at which you wake up and say, "Today's the day I start wearing a bra!" Instead, it's a more gradual decision. Once your breasts start developing, you may notice you feel a little self-conscious about the way they stick out from your shirt (remember, young breasts start out shaped kind of pointy). Or maybe all your friends are wearing bras, and you're starting to feel left out. If you play sports, you may notice an uncomfortable bouncing when you sprint down the field. And finally, some girls start wearing a bra when they're mom says,

"Hey, let's go bra shopping!" In the end, you need a bra when you feel like you'd like to wear one.

Q. What size bra should I buy?

A. Great question! Surveys show an astounding number of women walk around wearing bras that don't fit right simply because they've never been measured to find what size bra fits best. Bras come in sizes that include a number, like 32, and a letter, like B. The number is the size of your rib cage, or the band size of the bra. The letter is the size of your breasts, or the cup size of the bra. The best way to get a bra that fits just right is to have the saleslady measure you at the store—it's a totally free service, they do it all the time, and they can measure right over your clothes, so you don't need to feel shy or embarrassed.

You can also measure your size yourself or have a friend or family member help you out. Here's what to do:

1. Take a tape measure and measure around your ribcage, right below your breasts. Write down that number.

2. Add six inches to the number you got in step 1. If this number is even, that's your band size. If it's odd, subtract one inch (bands only come in even sizes) and that's your band size. For example, if your ribcage measures twenty-four inches, adding six gives you a size 30. If your ribcage measures twenty-five inches around, adding six gives you 31, an odd number. So subtract one, and you're a size 30, too.

3. Now figure your cup size. Wrap the tape measure around your chest, around your back and over the fullest part of your breasts, which is generally right across your nipples. Write that number down.

4. Subtract the number you got for your band size from the number you got in step 3 (for example, if your band size is 31, and your breast size is 32, you would subtract 31 from 32). The difference between your breast size and your band size is the cup size. Use the chart on page 163 to find your cup size letter.

Breast Size - Band Size Number	Cup Size
-1 or other smaller number	AAA
0	AA
1	A
2	B
3	C
4	D
5	DD

5. Put your band size number together with your cup size letter—for example, 28A or 32B—and you have your bra size!

No matter how carefully you've measured, always try a bra on before you buy it. Bras are like pants. One size in one brand may not fit the same as the same size in another brand. A well-fitting bra should be snug, but not supertight so you can't breathe or it digs into your shoulders, back, or boobs! The cups should fit smoothly over your breasts with no wrinkles or saggy spots. And your breasts should fit inside the cups without spilling out of the sides.

Q. How tight should the straps be?

A. The shoulder straps should be tight enough so that you feel supported—that is your breasts pretty much stay put instead of bouncing around—but not so tight that they dig into your skin or hurt your shoulders. Likewise, the band around your ribs should be snug, but not supertight. If you find your bra riding up in the back a lot, try fastening the hook one or two notches in. If it's squeezing into your back, fasten it farther out.

Q. There are a million styles to choose from. How do I choose?

A. The style of bra you pick depends on a lot of things. What kind of shirt are you wearing? What shape are your breasts? What style feels like "you?" Here's a rundown of the most popular bra styles and how they make your breasts appear:

- **Training bras.** No they don't train your breasts to grow bigger, sit, or heel. They simply get you used to wearing a bra. These are best for girls who would love to start wearing a bra, but don't have a lot to put in one yet.

- **Soft-cup bras.** When you want to wear a bra without looking too much like you're wearing a bra, the soft cup is the way to go. Like the name says, the cups are soft and usually seamless, so they make your breasts look very natural. They aren't as good at controlling bouncing, however, so if you're larger than a B cup, you might consider another style.

- **Underwire bras.** Girls with C cup or larger breasts might like underwires best. They're made with a curved bit of flexible wire sewn into the bottom of each cup, so they give you a little extra lift and support to hold your breasts in place. These can be soft-cup bras.

- **Padded bras.** You can buy all kinds of padded bras—some with thick padding all the way around, some with extra padding at the bottom for added "lift," and some with just some thin overall padding to give you more fullness. As you probably guessed, padded bras are designed to make your breasts look bigger.

- **Seamed bras.** Seamed bras have cups that are constructed out of a couple of pieces of material so they form your breasts into a firm, rounded shape. They look nice under sweaters and bulky clothes. But the seams show through T-shirts and other lightweight fabrics.

- **Demi bras.** Demi bras are the kind you see some celebrities like Madonna walking around in. The cups are cut super-low, like just above the nipples, so women can wear them under low-cut dresses. They're not exactly everyday wear, especially for large-breasted girls, since they make your boobs spill out over the top—probably not the look you're shooting for.

- **Push-up bras.** Though they've been around forever, the underwear company Victoria's Secret made these bras popular again. Push-up bras shove your breasts together and lift them way up, making you look superbusty. Push-up bras are meant to be glamorous, not exactly schoolday stuff.

- **Minimizer bras.** A lot of bras work hard to make small breasts look bigger. The minimizer is designed to do just the opposite—make large breasts look smaller. These bras compress your breasts closer to your body, so they don't stick out as far. Girls who have D cups or larger are sometimes more comfortable in minimizer bras.

- **Sports bras.** Sports bras are designed to hold your breasts in place while you run and jump. They look more like cut off tank tops than bras. And though they're designed for sports, you can wear them every day if you like, though they may be a little bulky under some shirts.

Q. I want to wear a bra, but I'm embarrassed. Can everyone tell I'm wearing one?

A. It depends on what you're wearing. If you wear shirts made out of a thick material or sweaters, then chances are no one will notice you're wearing a bra. But under lighter material shirts or T-shirts, it may be more obvious. Once you start wearing one for a while—and noticing all the other girls who are wearing bras, too—you'll probably feel much less self-conscious about people being able to tell.

Q. I'm totally flat chested, but I hate not wearing a bra when all my friends do. Is it stupid to wear a bra when you don't have anything to put in it?

A. It's not stupid at all. In fact, that's exactly what training bras are for—girls who want to wear a bra, but their bodies aren't quite ready. So go ahead and get one if you want one and it's okay with your mom. Or, you can wear a snug tank top or camisole under your shirts, so it looks like you're wearing something under your clothes, but it's not obvious what it is.

> "I am starting to develop, so I'm wearing a bra—
> and I like it!"
>
> **Britany, 11**

Q. Should I wear my bra when I sleep?

A. You *can* if you want to. But there's no reason to whatsoever. In fact, you'd probably be more comfortable without all those straps that shift and twist as you sleep.

Q. I've just started to develop breasts and feel very self-conscious. I want to wear a bra, but my mom says it's too soon. How can I convince her?

A. Your mom probably doesn't see your breasts as being as noticeable as you do. (We always think stuff on our own bodies is more obvious than it is to other people.) But that doesn't make you feel any better or mean you shouldn't try to convince her to buy some bras. Try explaining to your mom that even though it's early and you're not that big yet, that you feel really self-conscious at school, and it would make you feel much more comfortable to wear a training bra. If she understands how uncomfortable you're feeling, she'll be more likely to change her mind.

Q. Do I need a sports bra when I play sports?

A. It's a really good idea. Running around causes major bouncing, which can pull the connective tissues that support your breasts. Some experts think that can cause your breasts to sag more than they should. But more important, it's really uncomfortable and distracting to have your boobs jiggling all over the place when you're trying to concentrate on a game! There are basically two kinds of sports bra. The compression bra looks like a little tank top. It presses your breasts tight to your body so they can't move much. The encapsulation, or isolation, bra holds each breast separately in a supportive cup. For women with full C-cup breasts or larger, encapsulation is the way to go because they're better for minimizing bouncing. The only bummer about encapsulation bras is that they often look more like real bras, with hooks and adjustable straps, than compression sports bras. You wouldn't want to wear them by themselves without a T-shirt over them.

Q. I got my first bra just a few months ago, and it's already all stretched out and doesn't stay put. How can I make my next one last longer?

A. Hand washing your bras is really the best for them. But that's definitely a pain. Instead, try to protect them when you toss them in the washing machine. Always wash bras in cool or cold water. And try not to toss them in loose with all your other clothes, or they'll end up tangled up around your jeans and sweatshirts. Instead, throw your bras in a mesh bag called a lingerie bag and toss the bag in the wash. Once they're washed, it's generally a good idea to keep them out of the dryer, which can damage the elastic and cause them to shrink or fray. Hang them to dry instead. And finally, do yourself a favor and get more than one bra. By alternating through a couple of bras, they'll last longer.

Bras

Watch Out for Bad Bra Info!

If you spend any time on the Internet, you know that as useful as it can be for researching papers and keeping in touch with friends, it's also *filled* with rumors and bogus information. One rumor that continues to circulate on the Net is that bras cause cancer. A few years ago, a man and woman who were *not* doctors or medical scientists came up with a theory that bras cut off circulation from your lymph nodes (part of your immune system), which are under your arms, so toxins build up and cause breast cancer. That theory's been tossed in the trash by reputable medical professionals, but it still lingers on the Internet. If you hear it, don't sweat it. Even tight-fitting bras don't mess with your lymphatic system.

Check It Out!

Web site: www.x-chrom.com (a woman's sportswear site that offers advice on choosing the best sports bra for you; also includes stories about and interviews with inspiring active women)

Dieting

Too Much Fretting About Fat

Fact: Your body goes through growth and weight spurts during your preteen years. You get taller. You add a little weight. Sometimes, however, those growth and weight spurts don't happen in the order girls like. You may put on the pounds before the inches or the inches before the pounds, leaving you on a little bit of a seesaw when it comes to weight. But too many girls don't appreciate that puberty is a time for growth, not a time to be freaking because you think you're "fat." The result: They end up trying to diet—a bad idea for healthy development. Here's the scoop on "watching your weight."

"I don't know anyone my age who's been on a diet. But my mom and my grandma are both on diets. I'm happy with my own weight, though."

Kortni, 10

Q. My mom diets, why shouldn't I?

A. Honestly, there's a good chance your mom shouldn't be dieting either! Dieting means that you're depriving yourself of food for a period of time to lose weight. Once a diet stops, most people go back to eating like they used to and gain back all—if not more—of the weight they lost, that is, if they lost any. A better approach is to just eat healthfully, making sure to have fruits, vegetables, or both at every meal, and to exercise regularly. If you eat good food most of the time, with just a few sweets and some junk food now and then, you don't have to worry about your weight or "going on a diet."

What's more, although dieting isn't really healthy for either you or your mom, it's worse for you. Right now, you need all the good nutrition you can get to build the toughest, strongest bones you can. Not to mention that the rest of you—including your brain—is still developing, too. All that growth takes plenty of vitamins and minerals, especially calcium and iron—two nutrients dieting girls often get only skimpy amounts of. Girls who go on strict diets can end up with brittle bones, plus research shows they actually stunt their growth. Even if you don't diet enough to hurt your bones or your growth, you can end up with a lot of little unpleasant side effects—like dry hair, dull skin, fatigue, and general irritability from being hungry a lot. Maybe it's time that you *and* your mom ditch the diets and get on a healthy food kick instead.

Q. How can a diet hurt me if I don't do it long?

A. True, you can probably go on even a wacky diet of eating nothing but cucumbers and oatmeal for a few days and not hurt yourself long term—though you'll still feel pretty hungry, tired, and miserable for the time you're on it. But let's face it, who diets for just a couple days or even a week? Dieting becomes habitual. Some women end up losing and gaining weight on a merry-go-round of diets for their whole lives. It's a huge drag, as they don't ever learn to enjoy food without stressing all the time. Habitual dieting can also open the door to eating disorders like anorexia and bulimia (see Eating Disorders, page 183). And that's something you *definitely* don't want! The diet industry pulls in *multimillions* of dollars a year from people who get caught up in the dieting trap. Don't be one of them!

> "In the fifth grade, after someone made derogatory remarks about me, I became more aware of my weight. My New Year's resolution was to shed my extra layers. I put myself on crash diets, and when they ended in failure, I felt more miserable."

Melissa, 13

Q. What can I do instead of dieting to be sure I don't get fat?

A. Eat healthy foods, girl! Our country is swimming in so much junk food and supersized fast food that some people don't know what normal, healthful eating is anymore. Check out the food pyramid (see figure 13) and let that be your guide. Try to eat "whole foods" whenever you can. That means foods that you can recognize as a natural food that hasn't been overly processed. Pick vegetables, fruits, grains, beans, and lean meats over French fries, Ding Dongs, and hot dogs. If you follow the food pyramid and eat healthful, whole foods most of the time and junk food just occasionally, you don't need to worry about gaining excess weight.

Also, remember to listen to your body. It'll tell you when you're hungry and when you're full. So instead of grazing on chips and M&Ms just because you're bored and they're there, head outside to shoot some hoops or go read a book. And finally, don't let yourself get hungry to the point where you're ready to scarf down anything that doesn't move. If you know your day is going to be crazy, carry a healthful snack like a banana and some crackers.

Q. What's so bad about wanting to be the same size as my friends?

A. It's natural to want to fit in, especially with your close friends. But take a look around you. Healthy people come in all kinds

Food Guide Pyramid
A Guide to Daily Food Choices

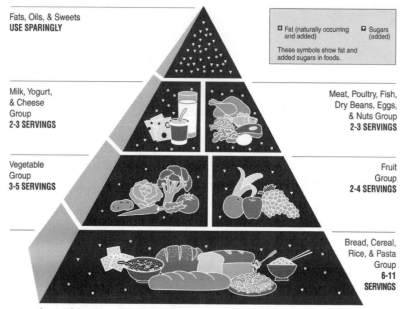

Fats, Oils, & Sweets
USE SPARINGLY

☐ Fat (naturally occurring and added)   ☑ Sugars (added)

These symbols show fat and added sugars in foods.

Milk, Yogurt, & Cheese Group
2-3 SERVINGS

Meat, Poultry, Fish, Dry Beans, Eggs, & Nuts Group
2-3 SERVINGS

Vegetable Group
3-5 SERVINGS

Fruit Group
2-4 SERVINGS

Bread, Cereal, Rice, & Pasta Group
6-11 SERVINGS

Source: U.S. Department of Agriculture/U.S. Department of Health and Human Services

Figure 13. Standard food pyramid.

of shapes and sizes. In fact, there are three specific body types that most people tend to be one of: Endomorphs (curvy), ectomorphs (slim) and mesomorphs (muscular). If you're born with a larger bone structure and curvy hips and shapely breasts, you won't turn yourself into a string bean no matter how much you diet. Also consider this: For every curvy girl who wishes she was skinny, there's a skinny girl who longs to have larger breasts and a more voluptuous figure. There's just no point in wasting a lot of time wanting what you don't have—instead, try being proud of and happy with what you *do* have.

Dieting

> "I knew someone who wasn't happy with her body, so she went on a diet. I don't think it's a good idea."

Britany, 11

Q. I understand why healthy, normal girls shouldn't diet. But I really am overweight. What can I do?

A. That's a good question. While many girls who are dieting are actually healthy, normal weights, there *is* a growing number of girls who struggle with real weight problems. Our culture is getting more sedentary—we spend less time playing outdoors and more hours parked in front of computers and the television. Plus, there's *tons* of junk food right at our fingertips and a Krispy Kreme at every corner. Still, it's not a good idea to diet during puberty. The best thing to do if you really think you have a weight problem is to talk to your parents and see a doctor. The doctor will be able to tell you how much, if any, weight you need to lose. She'll also be able to recommend specific healthy ways to gradually get down to the right weight for you and stay there.

Dieting

Diet Pill Dangers!

You already know to steer clear of diets—especially fad diets that have you eating some crazy food combinations, like grapefruits and cabbage soup, ten times a day to lose twenty pounds by tomorrow. But also avoid diet products like pills and herbs. Diet pills mess up your metabolism, and people have gotten sick and even died while taking them. Remember, if these products really worked miracles, everyone would take them and there'd be no more overweight people on the planet. They're a ripoff and potentially dangerous to your health.

Check It Out!

American Dietetic Association
216 West Jackson Boulevard
Chicago, Illinois 60606-6995
Phone: (312) 899-0040
Web site: www.eatright.org

Dieting

Drugs & Alcohol

Making Smart Decisions

If you haven't had to face it already, as you approach your teen years, you'll inevitably be faced with the issue of drugs and alcohol. Whether it's a friend who wants to try smoking cigarettes, someone at a party offering you a beer, or some kids in school talking about getting high or doing club drugs before a dance, part of growing up is learning how you feel about drugs and alcohol, then making intelligent decisions when the pressure is on. As with all tough situations in life, the more you know, the more confidently you can handle yourself and stand up for what you really want—or don't want—to do. Here's the scoop on using drugs and alcohol.

Q. Why do people drink and take drugs?

A. A lot of different reasons. Some people try them just because they want to feel cool or like they belong; others, because they're sad or depressed. And many people drink or take drugs because they want to feel good. Drugs temporarily alter your state of mind. They can make you feel really up and happy or mellow and carefree. Unfortunately, they can also backfire, making you careless, angry, or depressed. And even when a drug does make you feel good, the effect doesn't last. And you often end up feeling worse than when you started. That's why nasty fights often break out in bars and at parties. If you're ever thinking about trying drugs, it's important that you understand *why* you want to try them because often the real end result isn't what you wanted.

> "When I find out that kids are using drugs,
> I lose all respect for them."
>
> **Liz, 13**

Q. My parents drink. Why is it bad for me to drink?

A. You're at a time of life when everything about you is growing up and developing—including your brain. That makes it more susceptible to the damaging effects of alcohol than adults' brains are. What's more, you're at a much more vulnerable point in your life than your parents. They probably have a glass of wine with dinner or maybe a beer when they're with friends. Young people, especially young girls—often find themselves in dangerous situations when they drink because drinking impairs your judgment, leaving you vulnerable to abuse and making you more likely to do things you would otherwise not do. Alcohol is a factor in many sexual assaults and date rapes of teenage and college-age girls. Girls who drink are also more likely to have sex they later regret and unprotected sex, and they are at greater risk for catching sexually transmitted diseases like AIDS.

Drinking increases the likelihood that you'll get hurt in an accident, too. Use of alcohol and other drugs is a leading cause of death and injury (from car crashes, other accidents, and suicide) among teens.

Girls and women also have special health risks when they use alcohol. Women metabolize alcohol differently, so on the same amount of alcohol they get drunk faster and suffer the damaging effects of alcohol sooner than men do. Also, studies show drinking can raise your risk of breast cancer. And women who drink when they are pregnant can permanently damage their unborn babies.

Q. What do I do if I'm at a party and everyone is using drugs but me?

A. Honestly, you should probably leave. Aside from not being good for you, drugs are illegal, and police have a way of finding and busting parties, especially when there are a lot of noisy teens there. You don't want to call your parents from the police station and try to explain yourself.

You also need to realize that not everyone does do drugs. In fact, though it sometimes feels like "everyone" is doing it, the majority of preteens and teens *don't* use drugs. If you find yourself at parties and out with people who are frequently drinking or using drugs and are pressuring you to get involved, you should seriously consider if these are the kind of people you want as friends. Real friends will respect your decision not to drink or do drugs. After all, why should they care if you don't want to? In the end, you'll probably be happier finding friends you have more in common with.

Q. What are the most dangerous drugs?

A. That's an impossible question to answer. *All* drugs can be dangerous. And all drugs, including everyday stuff like beer and wine, are dangerous if you use them too much or too often. Here are some common drugs and their risks:

- **Alcohol.** Also known as booze, alcohol comes in a wide variety of forms, like beer, wine, liquor, and "alco-pops" (like wine coolers or sweet, blended drinks). It's one of the most commonly used drugs worldwide. It changes your perceptions and emotions, so you don't act like yourself. It increases your chances of getting hurt or killed in an accident and of having unwanted sex, and too much can damage important organs like your heart, liver, and brain.

- **Nicotine.** Found in tobacco products of all kinds—cigarettes, cigars, chewing tobacco—nicotine is a stimulant, so it gives you a "buzz," and it's *highly* addictive. Tobacco use is the leading cause of preventable death in this country. Tobacco users get heart disease, ulcers, and lung and other cancers. Also, studies show that adolescents who smoke are more likely to suffer depression than those who don't smoke. And, of course, it slows you down so you can't run or play very well, and everyone knows it gives you wrinkles and stained teeth.

- **Marijuana.** It goes by a lot of names, like weed, pot, and hash. The effects of pot vary from person to person, ranging from feeling giddy to feeling sleepy to feeling anxious and paranoid. Like alcohol, pot may be particularly damaging to still-developing brains. Long term, it causes the same damage to your heart, lungs, and other organs as smoking tobacco. Because marijuana "cigarettes" don't have filters on them, even more cancer-causing chemicals go directly to your lungs.

- **Ecstasy.** Also known as X, E, XTC, and MDMA, ecstasy is a popular "club drug" right now. It boosts energy, so people use it to stay up all night dancing, and it's supposed to enhance feelings of love and affection. Unfortunately, it can lead to permanent brain damage. It also can cause dehydration, and young girls have died at dances from heart failure while using it.

- **Amphetamine and methamphetamine.** Known also as ice, meth, crank, speed, and crystal. These drugs are powerful stimulants that raise your heart rate, give you energy, and in some people produce a "high" feeling. Speed is *very* addictive, and it's very easy to overdose on. Users have died from heart failure and burst blood vessels in the brain. Long-term use can lead to violent behavior and hallucinations.

- **Cocaine.** A *superaddictive* stimulant, cocaine is also referred to as blow, crack, coke, and snow. People use coke to feel energetic and alert. But the effects are very short-lived. Plus, you build up a tolerance to it, so it takes more and more to get the same high. Coke is very easy to overdose on, which can lead to seizures, heart attacks, and strokes, even in first-time users. Long-term use can damage your heart.

- **LSD.** Also called acid, LSD is a hallucinogen. (Other hallucinogens include mushrooms, or 'shrooms, and PCP, or angel dust.) Like the name implies, these drugs make you hallucinate—they mess up your senses so you see things that aren't there. The scary part of these drugs is there's no way to tell how it'll affect you. People have died thinking they can fly. Some people also become violent, injuring themselves or hurting others. Even worse, the affects can last for twelve hours. They can also cause heart failure.

- **Heroin.** Heroin, sometimes called smack or horse, can cause desperate addiction and is incredibly easy to overdose and die from, even the first time. People use it to get a feeling like a "rush of pleasure." But like any drug, the effects are short-lived, and the user needs more of the drug even just the second time to get the same affect. Users suffer from constipation and stomach cramps. People trying to quit go through painful physical withdrawal symptoms. Since heroin is usually injected with a needle, you also risk getting diseases like AIDS from dirty needles.

- **Ritalin.** Called vitamin R, or R-ball, Ritalin is the trade name for methylphenidate, a prescription drug used to help people with attention deficit disorder, or ADD. It's supposed to have a calming affect on hyperactive kids. Unfortunately, preteens and teens who don't need it have begun abusing it. Abuse of Ritalin can damage your central nervous system, possibly even lead to blood clots and some kinds of cancer.

- **Rohypnol** (row•HIP•nole). Also known as R-2, roofies, and the date rape drug, Rohypnol is the trade name for flunitrazepam and was originally created to be a medical sedative. Now it's being abused. This is one of the few drugs that people generally don't take out of choice—it's usually slipped into people's (most often, girls') drinks in bars and at parties without their knowing. Rohypnol makes you confused and out of it, sometimes even causing you to pass out. There have been cases of boys using it to take advantage of girls at parties. Too much can cause a coma. A good rule of thumb is not to drink anything if you don't know what's in it.

- **Nitrous oxide.** Usually called whippets, poppers, or laughing gas, nitrous oxide is a colorless, almost odorless gas that some dentists use. It makes you feel relaxed and giddy. Though it's pretty safe if used in a medical office, some people buy nitrous oxide to use it to get high. In this form, nitrous oxide (which is freezing cold) can cause cold damage to your lips and vocal cords. Long term it may cause brain damage.

- **Inhalants.** Believe it or not, some people will inhale glue, paint thinner, and even gasoline. It's a practice called *huffing,* and they do it to try to get a high feeling. These chemicals are extremely toxic, and huffing is way, way dangerous. Trying it just one time can cause sudden death. Other risks are nosebleeds and loss of control of your bodily functions, so you pee or have a bowel movement without meaning to. Long term, huffing can cause permanent brain damage.

"When I hear about kids doing drugs I get scared. When I was very little, my stepmom had me watch a movie about kids doing drugs, and it freaked me out a lot."

Ashlyn, 13

Q. I know a lot of people who have tried drugs and are fine. Is trying drugs just one time really that bad for me?

A. That's the tricky thing about trying drugs. Some people can try drugs once and not have anything bad happen to them. Others can get dangerously hooked after even one try, especially if they're trying a highly addictive drug like cocaine or heroin. Some drugs like "designer drugs" or "club drugs" can be very dangerous to try even once because they're made by people who may not know what they're doing. If you happen to get a drug from a bad batch, you could get very sick. Some people have even died after just one experience with bad drugs.

It's also important to remember that people usually don't try drugs just once. A lot of people start smoking cigarettes, drinking, or taking drugs just "occasionally" or "only on weekends." But before you know it, they're doing it once in a while during the week, too. Then it's every evening. The worst addictions sneak up on people who started out swearing they were just going to try it once. Addiction is a powerful physical and/or psychological need for a drug. And addictions don't just destroy *your* life, but they hurt your friends and family, too. Once you have an addiction, it's the hardest thing in the world to quit. Remember, nobody *ever* thinks that *they* are going to get addicted—yet somehow millions of people do.

The Dangers of Overdosing

One of the most dangerous things you can do—and something that is especially common in teens and young adults—is to drink a lot (like several drinks) or do a lot of drugs in one night or at one party in order to get really drunk or high. It's super-easy to overdose, which means you've poisoned yourself and could end up very sick and even die. If you ever see someone pass out from drinking or doing drugs, and they can't be woken up or they're having trouble breathing, call 9-1-1 right away. Young people die every year from drug overdoses and alcohol poisoning.

Check It Out!

National Council on Alcoholism and Drug Dependence (NCADD)
20 Exchange Place, Suite 2902
New York, New York 10005
Phone: (212) 269-7797
Help hotline: (800) NCA-CALL (622-2255)
Web site: www.ncadd.org (includes a section with stats and information just for kids)

Eating Disorders

Self-Destructive Dieting

In our appearance-obsessed society, it's tough—especially for girls—to not worry, even just a little bit, about weight. Sadly, some girls get so caught up in trying to be thin, they stop eating healthfully and develop eating disorders—dangerous patterns of eating, or not eating, that can make you terribly sick, not to mention very unhappy. Girls who develop eating disorders usually aren't overweight to begin with; they're healthy and kickin'. But because of their illness, that's not what they see in the mirror. They see fat, no matter how thin they are. Though eating disorders center around food and thinness, the real reasons girls develop these problems often have very little to do with their actual weight and more to do with how they feel about themselves and their relationships with people. Sometimes girls with eating disorders are punishing themselves or others. Sometimes they mistakenly believe they'll be a better person or more popular. Whatever the reason, eating disorders can permanently damage your health—some girls even die—so you need to take them seriously. Here's what you need to know about eating disorders, and how to avoid them.

Q. What is an eating disorder?

A. An eating disorder is an obsession with weight control that makes people behave in ways they can't control, like refusing to eat or trying to control their weight in other unhealthy, obsessive ways. Although boys can develop eating disorders, many more girls are affected. These problems usually happen to girls in their teens and early 20s, but younger girls can be affected, too. There are two major types of eating disorders:

1. **Anorexia.** Anorexia, short for *anorexia nervosa,* causes a girl to literally starve herself. A girl who has anorexia has no clue what she really looks like. While she may be nothing but skin and bones, she *sees* nothing but fat. She also will go to great extremes to avoid eating and may exercise excessively to burn off what little food she does eat. Anorexia is *very* serious—about 10 percent of girls who have the disease can die from it. Some of the physical symptoms include: severe weight loss, loss of hair, loss of periods, dry skin, fine hair growing on face and upper body, slow heart rate and low body temperature (always cold), constipation, bone loss, and kidney and heart problems (in the worst cases, even heart failure!). Psychologically, anorexia can cause mood swings and depression, even suicidal feelings; problems with sleeping; and, of course, obsession with food and maybe exercise.

2. **Bulimia.** Instead of starving themselves, girls with bulimia will do what is known as bingeing and purging. That is, they will eat a lot of food in one sitting, then they'll try to get rid of it by making themselves throw up or by taking laxatives that cause them to have excessive bowel movements. Girls who have bulimia can be tougher to spot, because, unlike girls who have anorexia, they're usually normal weight. But like girls who have anorexia, they perceive themselves to be fat. Like anorexia, bulimia can be fatal if it's not treated. Some common physical symptoms include: frequent weight gains and losses; loss of period;

eroded teeth (from stomach acids in their vomit); irregular heartbeat; sore throat; dry, cracked skin on hands (from forced vomiting); constipation; weakness; and dehydration. Psychologically, bulimia can cause an obsession with food, especially planning the next binge; secretive eating; depression; sleeping problems; anxiety; and mood swings.

Obviously, there's nothing fun about having an eating disorder. But girls who have them tend to feel trapped in them, and even though they may know deep inside that their behavior is hurting them and making them unhappy, they aren't able to change it.

Q. How do I know if I have an eating disorder?

A. It can be hard to spot an eating disorder in yourself. But if you're honest with yourself, you can usually tell if you have a problem that needs help. The following is a checklist adapted from The Renfrew Center, a nationally respected eating disorder treatment center. If you recognize these symptoms in yourself, you should talk to someone pronto:

- I feel guilty or ashamed about eating.

- I feel out of control.

- I feel depressed.

- I think I'm fat, even though everyone says I'm not.

- I obsess about food, eating, and/or calories.

- I exercise obsessively to lose weight.

- After meals and snacks, I make myself throw up or I take laxatives.

- I notice that I'm losing a lot of weight.

- I have irregular periods, or I have stopped getting my period.

Q. Does having an eating disorder mean I'm crazy?

A. No, you are not crazy. You have an illness. It's not your fault, and you shouldn't feel embarrassed. Too often, girls feel so ashamed of their behavior that they don't want to tell anyone, which means they don't get the help they need! Both physical and psychological factors play a role in eating disorders. The right therapy will help you through both.

Q. Can eating disorders be cured?

A. Yes. If you get treatment, you can expect to get better. You might even find that treatment does more positive things for you than just fix your eating disorder—although that's major! Treatment will help you get in touch with your feelings and understand why different emotions cause you to react and behave certain ways. You'll learn more about food and nutrition and how to eat healthfully. You'll get a better appreciation for your body and how to feed it. And since treatment is usually a family affair (your mom and dad go to sessions to learn, too), your parents get a chance to understand you better and you'll likely develop a better relationship. The sooner you seek treatment, the sooner you'll be on the road to feeling healthier, happier, and more in control.

Q. What if I want to eat normally, but I'm afraid of getting fat?

A. This is a common problem for girls with eating disorders. Being afraid of getting fat is a huge part of their condition, and it keeps them from getting help because they think getting better means getting fat. Treatment will *not* make you fat. If you are dangerously thin, you may need to gain a few pounds, but that won't make you fat; it will only help your body function normally and let your hair and skin become healthy and shiny again. Treatment will help you see how much better you actually look once you're eating again and how sick you looked when you were starving. If you're normal weight, that won't change with treatment, you'll just learn how to have a good relationship with yourself, with other people, and with food.

Part of getting better is learning to avoid having actual weight problems. It also helps you learn how to not worry about gaining weight. You learn to trust your body and listen to what it needs. You learn to eat when you're hungry and stop

Eating Disorders

when you're full. Instead of eating out of boredom or because you're angry or sad, you'll learn to deal with those emotions in other, more positive ways, like riding your bike or taking a walk. All that adds up to a healthy body and normal weight.

"I went to the doctor's office for a checkup. As I stepped onto the scale, I heard the nurse announce the number: 104. The words "Fatty, fatty, two-by-four" swirled through my mind. I cut my meal sizes in half and avoided all junk foods. Kids at school started telling me that I was "so thin and pretty." I absolutely loved this new attention. I felt incredibly strong-willed knowing I could resist urges toward eating and felt that others, who ate a lot, were weak and disgusting. As I kept losing weight, my mom and dad told me I looked grotesque with all my bones jutting out and my skin blotchy. They took me to a doctor who said I was dehydrated, hypothermic, nutritionally depleted, and that I had anorexia nervosa. My journey has been a long one and is not yet over. My goal is to one day use the knowledge I have gained from my disease to help someone. Whether it is one person or ten, I will be satisfied. I know that I am strong and capable of defeating anorexia."

Melissa, 13

Q. What should I do if I think a friend has an eating disorder?

A. Talk to her about your concerns. Say, "I've seen that you've stopped eating [or whatever the behavior is] and I'm worried about you. I think you should get some help." You should also tell an adult. This may feel like snitching, but an eating disorder is a problem that is too big for you and your friend alone.

Many girls who get treated end up getting help because their friends step in and tell a guidance counselor, teacher, or parent. Though your friend may be mad at you at first, most girls end up still being friends in the end. You're doing something very positive for your friend, and she'll realize it when she's better.

Watch Your Words!

It's easy to get caught up in the crowd and start praising people who look thin and putting down people who aren't, but don't do it! Likewise, if your girlfriends are sitting around ragging on their own bodies, saying things like "I'm so fat," don't chime in; change the subject instead. All this bad body talk can contribute to eating disorders—maybe even your own if it makes you feel bad about yourself. Instead, focus on the stuff that really matters, and try to find something positive to say about everyone, including yourself!

Check It Out!

American Anorexia Bulimia Association, Inc.
165 West 46th Street, Suite 1108
New York, New York 10036
Phone: (212) 575-6200
Web site: www.aabainc.org

The Renfrew Center
475 Spring Lane
Philadelphia, Pennsylvania 19128
Phone: (800) RENFREW (736-3739)
Web site: www.renfrewcenter.com

Fitness & Sports

Playing for Life!

Your body is the one machine that gets better the more you use it. The more you run, bike, swim, play sports, hike, and dance, the stronger your heart and lungs, the more solid your bones and the healthier your body will be overall. Though you don't usually worry about stuff like cancer, heart disease, and diabetes now, living an active life fights these and all kinds of other diseases. Exercise gives you better muscle tone, which looks great, and gives you the energy to participate in sports and fun of all kinds. What's more, studies show that girls who play sports feel better about their bodies, are less likely to use drugs or become pregnant, and are more likely to further their education after high school. Plus, staying fit is fun! Here's what you need to know about the world of exercise.

Q. What is fitness?

A. Fitness is the physical ability to engage in life. It lets you walk up stairs, play outside, and do regular activities, like carrying bags and planting flowers, without huffing and puffing or feeling wiped out. The core of fitness lies in the center of your

189

chest—your beating heart. See, your heart is actually a muscle. Though it's only about the size of your fist, your heart powers your whole body, pumping blood and sending oxygen to every muscle from your eyelids to your pinky toes. To do that, your heart beats about sixty times a minute! That means you need to keep it strong. Since your heart is growing right now along with the rest of you, this is a great time to help make it as healthy and powerful as it can be. Experts recommend that kids get at least thirty minutes of exercise every day—but they say it's even better if you get an hour or two of regular activity and play, including easy stuff like walking (all that walking at school and the mall counts!) as well as more energetic activity like playing soccer and other sports. It's okay to take a day off now and then to be a slug, of course. The idea is to get into a habit of doing something physical most days of the week.

"I don't play sports, but I do cheerleading because it keeps me busy and prevents me from getting lazy."

Tara, 13

Q. What kind of exercise should I be doing?

A. That's an easy one—whatever you like! If you hate running, no point in starting because you won't keep it up—you would probably look for every excuse in the world to bag it. That's why it's a good idea to try all kinds of activities so you can find out what you like. Think about all the stuff people do for fun: rock climbing, mountain biking, hiking, swimming, basketball, skateboarding, gymnastics, dancing, yoga, kayaking, golfing, tennis, Rollerblading, surfing, snowboarding, and so on! Try it all. You're bound to find something you love!

Remember, too, that variety rules when it comes to working out. Ideally, you should include activities that provide three distinct fitness benefits:

- **Cardiovascular.** Aerobic exercise, like jogging, bicycling, and dancing, provides what is known as cardiovascular benefits. That means it strengthens your heart and lungs.

- **Strengthening.** Muscle-building exercises, like swimming, yoga, and rock climbing, build lean tissue and keep your body strong and looking toned.

- **Flexibility.** Though you're probably plenty flexible now, your muscles and connective tissues (the tissues that connect muscle to bone and bone to bone) become less elastic over time, so it's important to do stretching exercises, like yoga or the simple stretches you do before and after playing sports, regularly.

Here are some tips for stretching:

- **Go easy.** Stretching shouldn't hurt! Lean into your stretch slowly just to the point where you feel the stretch (that is, it's a little uncomfortable, but *not* painful). You can hurt yourself if you stretch too fast or forcefully.

- **Hold it steady.** Once you're at the point where you feel the stretch, hold it steady right there for about fifteen seconds. Don't bounce or bob up and down—that can actually make muscles tighter.

- **Be thorough.** Stretching isn't as exciting as playing, but it's just as important, so take your time and hit every major muscle. Your body will thank you later!

Q. Do girls lift weights?

A. You bet! Weight lifting helps strengthen the muscles around your shoulders, knees, and elbows, so you can play sports more safely. It also builds bones, which is very important for young women in their peak bone-building years. And contrary to what you might think, it won't give you big, bulky muscles like Arnold Schwarzenegger. Soccer stars like Mia Hamm lift weights, as do swimsuit models like Rebecca Romjin-Stamos. And they certainly don't look like boys!

Fitness & Sports

Even though lifting weights is very good for you, it's not recommended for very young girls because their bones are still growing. So you should probably wait to hit the dumbbells. But once you're in your teens, you can usually start to lift safely, especially if you play sports. It's important that you get professional instruction from a coach or trainer before you start.

"I stay active by taking almost four hours
of dance classes a week."

Liz, 13

Q. Will puberty affect how I play sports?

A. Maybe, but not necessarily in a bad way. Some of the transitions, such as getting taller, growing breasts, or developing hips, may make you feel awkward sometimes until you get used to your new body. But as you get bigger, you can probably play many sports better because your muscles are stronger, and you'll have more endurance so you can play longer.

The one potential pitfall girls in particular have to watch out for is knee injuries. As your hips widen during puberty, the angle at which your leg bones connect to your knees changes, placing extra strain on the knees. Unfortunately, your leg muscles usually don't develop as fast as these other changes, so they don't help support and protect your knees as much as they should. The result: Girls who play sports, especially those that involve a lot of running, jumping, and cutting, are four to six times more likely than boys to injure their anterior cruciate (pronounced KRU·shee·ate) ligament (the connective tissue that runs behind your kneecap, connecting your shin bone to your thigh bone). To protect yourself, be sure your coach teaches you to jump and land properly—if that hasn't happened yet, ask to be shown how. Also, ask your coach for some age-appropriate exercises (remember very young girls shouldn't do heavy strength training) to strengthen the leg muscles that support your knees.

Q. What if my coach is mean, or I think my teammates are too serious?

A. Sports and games are supposed to be fun. But they're also competitive, so it's easy to understand why everyone playing also wants to win. The trick is balancing the competitive desire to kick butt with the love of playing the game just to play. Some players and coaches do that balancing act better than others. If your coach seems mean, he or she might just be acting tough to try to motivate you to practice and play the best you can. Also, that's how some coaches learned to coach when they played the game in school. Understanding why someone acts a certain way can help you take it less personally. If the coach seems mean for real, though, you might consider talking it over with your parents. They might have ideas for fixing the situation or making the game more fun for you again.

If everyone around you seems to be taking the game more seriously than you, and it's upsetting you, you might want to re-think being on the team. Some girls love team sports because they get a kick out of the camaraderie, team spirit, and sense of accomplishment that comes from being part of a group. Others find the pressure a little too intense to be fun. That's perfectly okay, and you don't have to give up athletics just because you feel that way. There are plenty of individual sports, like tennis, track and field, cross country, swimming, and golf. In these sports, even though you're technically part of a team, you're mostly competing for yourself. Or you can just find a solitary activity, like yoga, cycling, jogging, or dancing, that you enjoy.

Q. How can I keep from getting hurt in sports?

A. Accidents and injuries will always be a risk when you play sports. But you can definitely decrease your risk for getting hurt. *Always* wear the protective equipment recommended for whatever sports you play or activities you do. Helmets, shin guards, knee, elbow, and wrist pads, and mouthpieces may seem like a pain in the butt sometimes, but they save your vulnerable bones and joints from getting smashed when you hit the ground hard or when a ball—or another player—whacks into you full force.

You also can protect yourself by carefully following your coach's instructions on warming up and stretching. And practicing tricky maneuvers before actually using them in the game can help you master proper technique and leave you less likely to get hurt in the heat of competition.

And finally, always drink plenty of water. Dehydration can make you clumsy during your activity and more likely to get hurt. Drink before your games, during breaks, and after you're done. If you're going to be playing more than an hour or so, especially if it's hot outside, you should consider bringing some sports drink, like Gatorade, too, so you can put back some of the essential minerals you sweat out.

"The worst thing about being a girl is having boys make fun of you for being bad at sports."

Samantha, 9

Q. Why do I sweat when I exercise?

A. Whenever you exercise, your body creates heat. Without some release, you would overheat quickly, and would have to stop playing. Sweating is your body's cooling system. When you sweat, moisture comes out of the pores on your skin. As that moisture evaporates from your skin into the air, you feel cooler. Though you can't—and shouldn't—stop yourself from sweating, you *can* make it more comfortable. Avoid plain cotton shirts when exercising. Cotton can't release moisture fast enough when you're sweating, so you'll lose that nice evaporating and cooling effect. Better to choose the new high-tech fabrics that wick moisture away from your skin and dry quickly. All major sport brands, like Nike and Adidas, make good athletic shirts and shorts. Look for fabrics like CoolMax and Dri-Fit. Also, if you have long hair, pull it back in a ponytail or up in a bandana to allow your forehead and neck to cool off—those are prime spots where sweat collects!

Stay Fit and Healthy!

Sometimes the same sports that should be good for you can end up having negative side effects. In some sports, especially sports that emphasize a certain body type, like gymnastics, skating, and dancing, you can feel pressure to train very, very hard and to maintain a small, lean build. This can lead girls to not eat enough or develop eating disorders (see page 183). Unnaturally low body weight combined with excessive exercise can delay puberty if you haven't already started it, and it can throw a serious kink in the works if you have. Girls who have started menstruating can stop having their periods, which is a sign that your body is not able to develop naturally. The result can be stunted growth and poor bone development that can leave you with brittle, easily broken bones—certainly not something an athlete ever wants! If you're an athlete and have missed more than two periods in a row or have not yet begun to menstruate or develop breasts and pubic hair even though you're in your preteen or early teen years, you should talk to your parents about it and see a doctor who specializes in treating athletes. Your coach can probably recommend someone. If you're comfortable with it, you should also tell your coach about what's happening with you, so he or she can help you eat and practice in healthier ways.

Fitness & Sports

Check It Out!

American College of Sports Medicine
401 W. Michigan Street
Indianapolis, Indiana 46202-3233
Phone: (317) 637-9200
Web site: www.acsm.org

American Council on Exercise
P.O. Box 910449
San Diego, California 92191-0449
Phone: (858) 535-8227
Web site: www.acefitness.org

Fitness & Sports

First Gynecology Exam

Staying Healthy . . .
Inside and Out!

ike your teeth, eyes, heart, and lungs, your sexual organs and parts need regular checkups to make sure they're healthy and functioning properly. This can be done by a special doctor called a gynecologist or by a family doctor or nurse who performs gynecology exams. It's perfectly natural to be nervous about being checked out "down there." But these medical professionals see as many female body parts as shoe salespeople see feet, so it's no big deal. And once you see how simple the checkup is, you'll soon realize that there's nothing to be worried about! Here's what you need to know.

Q. When should I have my first gynecological exam?

A. As a rule of thumb you should have your first exam when you're eighteen if you haven't been sexually active. If you become sexually active, you need to have a gynecology exam at that point. Because of all the changes that come with puberty, girls in their teens are at a higher risk for sexually transmitted diseases, and of course, there's always the risk of getting pregnant. So it's important to see a doctor to help keep you safe and healthy.

Q. How can I find a doctor?

A. One easy way is going to the same doctor your mom goes to. Your mom's doctor already knows your family history, which is a benefit because many characteristics and conditions run in families. If it makes you uncomfortable to see your mom's doctor or if you want to see a doctor privately, look for teen-friendly clinics. There are often school-based health centers where you can get care. The nurse at school can probably help you find one. Remember, though, if you think something is wrong medically or you're concerned about your sexual health, your parents really should know. It may feel scary and awkward, but they know more about sexual stuff than you might give them credit for (you're here, aren't you?), and they can help you through it.

Q. Do I have to take off my clothes?

A. Yep. The doctor will tell you to undress from the waist down and to unhook your bra if you're wearing one. Some doctors may simply ask you to remove all your clothes and slip into a gown that they have available. This feels freaky, no question. Even adults get uncomfortable. But don't bug out. Your doctor sees hundreds of naked bodies, and to them, it's no more exciting than being a mechanic and looking under a car hood.

Q. What if the doctor is a man?

A. Again, it's important to remember that he's not looking at you in any sexual way. He's just a person who knows a lot about reproductive parts. Also, any time you have a man performing your exam, a female nurse or other female health professional will stay in the room with you during the exam to make you feel more comfortable. If you're still not happy, it's perfectly okay to say you're not comfortable and that you would rather have a female doctor. But if the gender of your doctor is very important to you, it's best to find out if the doctor is a man or woman *before* your appointment.

Q. What kind of tests will the doctor perform?

A. First the doctor will perform the all-important "talk test." That is, he or she will chat with you to find out how you're doing generally. The doctor will ask about your health history, if you or anyone in your family has had any diseases or medical conditions, and will also want to know if you've started to menstruate, when you got your first period, and what your periods are like—are they long or short? Heavy or light? That kind of thing. And finally, he or she will ask if you're sexually active. If you are, it might be tempting to shake your head no because you're afraid of getting in trouble, but don't. Your doctor needs you to be honest in order to offer birth control advice and protect your health. This person is not trying to pry or judge you, and, if you're over the age of twelve, won't tell your parents.

Once you're done talking, the physical part of the exam starts. The doctor will ask you to lie back on a special table and either rest your feet in special holders called stirrups, or place them on an attached ledge with your legs spread. This is to see your vulva and easily perform the internal exams. These are the tests you can expect:

- **Visual check.** The first thing the doctor wants to do is look inside your vaginal canal to check for redness, inflammation, or any other signs of infection or problems. As you know, your vagina walls naturally touch each other, making it impossible to just peer in there. So before any tests start, the doctor will insert a tubular instrument called a speculum (SPEC·you·lum) that opens the walls of your vagina. That way the doctor can see in. Speculums are hard and usually cold, so it's not the most comfortable experience, but it's not painful. Breathe deep and try to calm your mind and relax your muscles. You'll feel better.

- **Pap smear.** After the visual check, with the speculum still in place, the doctor will perform a Pap smear. This is mainly a test to check for cervical cancer, though it also can be used to check for some sexually transmitted diseases. The doctor will insert an instrument that looks like a little brush on the end of a stick (or sometimes like a long Q-tip) into your vagina and rub it on your cervix to take a cell sample, which will then be put on a slide or in a vial to send to a laboratory for testing. The Pap test doesn't hurt, but you may feel some uncomfortable pressure while your cervix is rubbed, and you may have a spot or two of blood afterward.

- **Pelvic exam.** Once the Pap smear is taken, the doctor will remove the speculum (whew!), and start the final below-the-waist test—the pelvic exam. Wearing gloves, the doctor will insert a few fingers of one hand into your vagina, while pressing on the top of your lower abdomen with the other. The doctor is actually feeling your internal organs! By doing this he or she can feel if there's any swelling or unusual growths. This definitely feels a little weird, but, again, it shouldn't hurt. If it does, you should tell the doctor. Sometimes the doctor will finish this exam with a digital rectal exam. That means the insertion of a gloved finger into your rectum to check for any abnormalities there. Don't let it gross you out. It's done in a few seconds, and it's a standard test for your health.

- **STD screen.** This test isn't part of every gynecological exam, but if you or your doctor is concerned about sexually transmitted diseases that can't be detected from your Pap smear sample, the doctor may also order a blood test. Just a little blood is drawn and taken to a lab.

- **Breast exam.** Your gynecological exam also involves a breast check. Some doctors do breast exams first, while others save them for last. The doctor will feel your breasts for unusual lumps and will pinch your nipples to check for discharge (any fluid that comes out). The doctor will also explain how to check your breasts yourself—something you should do each month (see page 17).

- **Quick vital check.** And finally, the doctor will give you a basic once-over to assess your general health. He or she will feel the glands around your throat to make sure nothing's swollen and listen to your heart and lungs with a stethoscope. You'll probably also be weighed and have your blood pressure taken. It all sounds like a lot, but it's done before you know it and you have peace of mind, knowing that you're in good health.

Q. What if I have my period?

A. Make another appointment. Try to schedule one sometime in the middle of your cycle. Having your period can mess up your Pap smear results, so there's no sense doing it then.

Q. Will the doctor tell my parents about the exam?

A. That depends. If you're over the age of twelve, the doctor will keep your exam confidential if you wish. And you can certainly feel safe asking your doctor questions privately without worrying that he or she will tell your parents. But if something is wrong, you really should confide in your mom and dad. For one thing, you'll need some kind of treatment, which you probably would need your parents to pay for. Also, the exam itself costs money and someone has to pay for it. If you're covered by your parents' insurance, they'll receive an itemized bill from the insurance company showing all the tests you had done that day (although not the results). So it's best to be up front with them.

Make It an Annual Event!

Once you have your first gynecological exam, you should go for a checkup every year. A lot can happen in twelve months, and an annual exam is an easy way to be sure everything stays A-okay.

Check It Out!

American College of Obstetrics and Gynecology (ACOG)
409 12th Street, S.W.
Washington, D.C. 20090-6920
Phone: (202) 638-5577
Web site: www.acog.com

Makeup

A Little Goes a Long Way

As you start going through all the changes of becoming an adult, it's perfectly natural to start having interests in some adult things, like makeup. Experimenting with makeup is definitely fun. But it can also make you look too old, or just plain goofy if you wear a lot of it or get dolled up to go play soccer. The trick is to choose the right cosmetics and to know how—and when—to wear them. Here's a guide.

"One of the best things about being a girl is that you can do pretty things with your hair and makeup every morning. Boys don't get that pleasure."

Ashlyn, 13

Q. When is it okay to start wearing makeup?

A. There is no one magical age when society says it's okay for girls to put on lipstick and blush. Some people think it's okay for junior high girls, while others think definitely not before you hit high school. When adults are concerned about your wearing makeup, often what they're worried about is that you'll look older than you are. For instance, a twelve-year-old girl who has hit puberty can look fifteen or sixteen if she starts wearing makeup. While that may sound cool to you, the unwanted sexual attention you can end up getting from older boys who think you're older, too, *definitely* is not. Plus, makeup can be a real pain for active young girls (and women, too!), because it can smear and run if you play sports or run around. You need to take all this stuff into consideration before you decide if you want to start wearing makeup regularly. You also need to talk it over with your mom. Once you reach a decision, the best thing you can do is to wear makeup that is appropriate for your age— that is, don't just dig into your mom's stash. Get a few items that will give you the fresh punch of color you want without making you look like you're trying to be older than you are.

Q. Whenever I put on makeup, it looks too dark. What kind of makeup is best for looking good without looking "made up?"

A. This is a way common mistake among young girls. There's one golden rule for makeup at any age, but especially for young skin: *Less is more.* One of the things that gets girls into trouble is that they try to mimic hot looks they see in magazines and movies. Professional makeup artists, actresses, and models will all tell you—what looks good in a picture or on the screen often looks terrible in real life. It's okay to get inspired by those looks, but when you try them yourself, you need to tone them down so you look more natural and less like a clown. Here are some professional tips:

- **Foundation.** Foundation is a kind of makeup that is worn over your entire face to even out skin tone. It's too heavy for most girls to wear straight out of the bottle. If you have blemishes or red spots that you want to cover, use a little concealer (you can buy a cover-up stick in any drug store) that is slightly lighter than your skin tone. Apply a dab of the concealer over your pimple or blemish. Then pour some foundation on a little dish and mix it with water so you have about ½ water, ½ makeup (if your skin is dry, you can use moisturizer instead of water). Then rub a light layer of this mixture on your face with your fingertips. This will give you a nice smooth, shimmery look without making you look or feel all made up. You can get foundation that has sunscreen in it, which will help protect your face from the sun's rays.

- **Eye makeup.** It's super-easy to overdo eye makeup, so be careful. Forget black liquid eyeliner. It may be okay for singers in music videos, but it looks awful in real daylight. Instead, stick to adding just a little color if you want to punch up your eyes. Try an eyegloss stick. They're totally sheer and give a nice tint instead of a big smudge of dark color.

  Some girls wear mascara to make their eyelashes thicker, but this can be more trouble than its worth. Mascara that isn't waterproof tends to smudge under your eyes—hardly attractive! And mascara that is waterproof is tough to remove. If you do wear mascara, use just one or two swipes to avoid the fake eyelash look.

- **Lip color.** Many lipsticks will be way too heavy for your naturally fresh face. Instead, try tinted lip balms. Chapstick even makes some. They provide protection for your lips so they don't dry out. Plus, they smell good, usually taste good, and you get a fresh tint of color. A common mistake many girls make is lining their lips with a lip pencil, then filling in with lipstick. This almost never works and ends up looking way overdone.

- **Blush.** For special occasions, you may want a little color in your cheeks. You can use a blush stick. But again, stick to a light, sheer shade. Put just a dab on the "apple" of your cheeks (the full part of your cheeks at the front of your face on either side of your nose), and lightly rub it around so you have just a hint of rosiness.

Makeup

Q. I want to wear makeup, but my mom won't let me. What can I do?

A. Talk to her. Think about why you want to wear makeup. Is it because you have some blemishes you want to cover? Your mom might understand that and say okay. Is it because you just think it would be fun? Maybe she'll compromise with some glittery lip balm. Have a heart-to-heart with her. If you don't pitch a fit and do your best to calmly explain why it's important to you, she's more likely to hear your side of things. Also, tell her what you have in mind when you say makeup. She may be picturing ruby red lips and dark blue eye shadow, when all you want to wear is some pink lip gloss and a little hair glitter. She may still say no, in which case you'll just have to respect her wishes and wait a little longer, but she's more likely to compromise if she knows where you're coming from and what you have in mind.

Also, there are plenty of things you can do to jazz up your looks without wearing makeup. Experiment with fun hair styles. Wear hair jewelry. You can even have your eyebrows groomed the same place you get your hair cut. They remove stray hairs and give your brows a nice shape.

"One of the coolest things about being a girl
is being able to do lots of different looks,
like makeup and clothes."

Britany, 11

Q. Does wearing makeup cause wrinkles? I heard it ages your skin.

A. Makeup won't age your skin, but if you don't remove it properly every night, it can have some side effects that aren't so pretty. Having makeup on your skin 24/7 blocks your pores and contributes to pimple breakouts. Use a skin cleanser and wash your makeup off every night before you go to bed. Also, give your face a chance to breathe and take a day off from wearing makeup now and then.

Share Makeup, Not Disease!

It's fun get together with friends and make each other up. Just be careful when swapping and sharing makeup. Using each other's cosmetics, especially eye and lip makeup, is an easy way to spread bacteria and infections. Instead, use Q-tips to put on makeup and toss 'em when you're done. If you're going to share lip gloss, wipe the stick of gloss off with a tissue first.

Check It Out!

Web site: www.theteenzone.com (offers tips on everything from fashion to cosmetic ideas)

Makeup

Nutrition

Fab Foods to
Feed Your Growing Self

survey of seventh- and eighth-grade girls confirms it—chicks dig junk food. But while nachos and ice cream may rule, a survey by Just Kid, of Stanford, Connecticut, shows that some girls (and boys) also try to make nutritious choices about what they munch on. More than 70 percent of kids surveyed gave a resounding "Yes!" when asked if they love to eat junk food. About 30 percent preferred healthy snacks to the sugary, salty, and high-fat sort. While everyone dips into chips now and then—and that's totally okay!—it's important to make most of your meals balanced and healthful. Forming good eating habits now will give you more energy, fend off disease, and make it easier to keep a healthy weight in your twenties, thirties, and beyond. What's more, eating right feels good. A diet filled with whole grains; juicy fruits; and bright, colorful veggies leaves your hair shiny, your skin healthy, and your body strong. Here's what you need to know.

Q. How much food do I need every day?

A. Growing up takes a lot more energy than most girls think. While you may hear of adults counting calories, that's not a good idea for girls. Growing girls between the ages of seven and fourteen can need more than twice as much daily energy (which is all calories are—energy) than an adult woman. The best plan is to eat three balanced meals and a couple snacks each day to keep your body fueled and your energy levels high. Remember that although chips and candy bars give you plenty of instant energy (can you say sugar?), the energy wears off quickly, and on top of it, they're not very nutritious. So try to choose healthful foods when you can. Refer to the food pyramid on page 172 for guidance on the best foods to eat every day.

Also, the National Cancer Institute recommends aiming to eat "five a day" every day—that is, at least five servings of fruits and five servings of vegetables. Fruits and vegetables can help fend off diseases and keep you in top health.

"I like really weird foods—my favorites are lobster and sushi. I like vegetables, and I eat salad almost every day."

Liz, 13

Q. I'm not hungry in the morning. Do I really need breakfast?

A. You don't need the lumberjack's special if you're not into food in the morning, but you definitely should eat something. A lot of studies have shown that kids who don't eat in the morning don't perform as well on tests and quizzes, even if they feel fine. It's because your brain doesn't have all the energy it needs to perform its best. Also, people who eat breakfast are more likely to maintain a healthy weight, because breakfast helps "wake up" your energy systems for the day. Some researchers have found that people who live to be a hundred years old tend to be regular breakfast eaters. (Sure, there are probably a lot of other reasons they live to be 100, too, but it's still cool that breakfast might contribute!) So even if you're not particularly hungry, there are a lot of reasons to grab a breakfast bar or a small bowl of cereal to start your day.

Nutrition

Q. Can I just take vitamins if I don't like vegetables?

A. No way. Even though *The Jetsons* predicted that we'd be popping pills instead of food one day, that's not the case today and probably won't be for a long time, if ever. (Besides, who would want to give up food?!) Vitamin and mineral supplements like Flintstones, Bugs Bunny, Centrum, and many other multivitamins can make sure you get 100 percent of the important nutrients you need every day. But food has a lot of stuff in it that vitamin pills don't.

For one thing, veggies are an excellent source of fiber. You need plenty of fiber to keep your digestive system working smoothly and maybe prevent certain kinds of cancers as well as heart disease. Veggies and fruits also contain something else that keeps you healthy—*phytochemicals.* The plants we eat contain hundreds, maybe thousands, of chemicals that scientists are just beginning to understand. But so far, researchers know that the same chemicals that make tomatoes red and grapes purple also work in our bodies fighting diseases of all kinds and keeping us healthy. You can't get all the phytochemicals your body needs from pills, only from foods. If you don't like vegetables, maybe you haven't tried them cooked in different ways. Grilled or roasted veggies taste very different from steamed or raw ones. Or you can try them in a spicy, exotic sauce like they do in Chinese and Indian restaurants. Before you dismiss them, give them a chance—you might be surprised!

Q. I eat junk food and feel okay. Do I really need to worry about nutrition?

A. Yep, you do. If you could look inside your body, you'd see a lot of amazing things going on. Your bones are building more now than they will at any other time in your life, so they need calcium. Your body is making more blood for menstruation—so you can have a baby one day—and that takes iron. And you're turning into a woman in a dozen other different ways, from growing breasts to producing eggs, which requires zinc. Be-

Nutrition

cause of poor eating habits—lots of junk food and soda—girls your age routinely miss out on getting adequate amounts of those three essential nutrients. Though you may not feel the consequences now, weak bones can put you at risk for osteoporosis (a disease that makes your bones thin and brittle, which, in turn, means they break easily) down the road. Low iron can make you tired and draggy. And too little zinc leaves your immune system vulnerable to colds and sickness.

What's more, researchers see more and more that what you eat now has a big impact on your health later on. Lots of junk food can cause your arteries to start hardening, even at a very young age. Down the road, poor eating habits can also lead to health woes like diabetes and cancer. Now's the time to get smart and eat food that is good for you—and the thing is, it tastes good, too.

"My favorite food is what every girl or boy likes—junk! I love junk—anything from chips to candy to ice cream. I also enjoy fruit very much."

Ashlyn, 13

Q. Is it safe to be a vegetarian?

A. Yep. But if you're going to make the change to not eating meat (and your mom or dad isn't vegetarian), it's a good idea to see a registered dietitian to be sure you're getting all the protein and other important nutrients you need.

There are also many different kinds of vegetarian diets. Some people just have a "beef" with red meat, but eat chicken and fish. Others are okay with eggs and milk, but not any kind of meat. Some vegetarian diets are easier to deal with, especially when you're out at a restaurant or eating at the school café. Others take more work. Here are some of the most common types:

- **Semivegetarians.** This is the most common bunch. These folks basically eat everything but red meat and pork. They eat mostly plant foods, plus some dairy, eggs, fish, and poultry.

- **Pescovegetarians.** Sometimes jokingly called "fishaterians," this group is also very common. They forgo red meat, poultry, and pork, but include fish and other seafood, along with plant foods, dairy, and eggs.

- **Lactovegetarians.** This group avoids meats, fish, poultry, and eggs, but does include dairy in their veggie diet.

- **Ovovegetarians.** Similar to lactovegetarians, ovovegetarians avoid meats, fish, and poultry. However, they eat no dairy but do eat eggs.

- **Ovo-lactovegetarians.** You guessed it. This group avoids all meats, fish, and poultry, but happily munches on eggs and dairy.

- **Vegans.** These folks eat nothing of animal origin, which includes dairy, eggs, and even honey. It can be tough to be a vegan, since so many products—like cakes, breads, desserts, sauces, dressings, and other everyday foods—include butter and milk products. But again, a dietitian can help direct you toward a large array of nonanimal foods that are tasty and healthful.

If you're going to choose to be a vegan, you will need to supplement vitamin B_{12}, a vitamin prevalent in animal foods. If you don't get enough B_{12}, you may find yourself feeling sick. All vegetarians should be sure to include a lot of nuts, nut butters, dried fruits, and seeds as well as meat substitutes, like soy foods and beans.

Though you can technically eat nothing but pasta and potato chips and call yourself a vegetarian, that's pretty lame and not at all healthy. Go with your mom, buy a few vegetarian cookbooks, and explore the possibilities open to you. Use this special vegetarian food pyramid (see figure 14) as your guide for what to eat day to day.

Nutrition

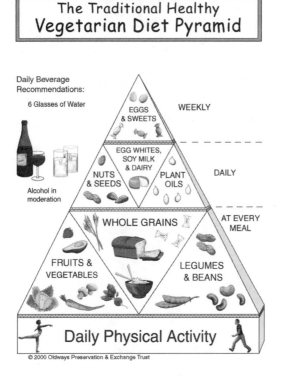

Figure 14. Vegetarian food pyramid.

Q. What kind of diet should I eat to lose weight?

A. None. Sorry, but now's the time for developing, not dieting. If you really do need to lose weight, you should talk to your parents and your doctor so you can do it in a healthful way. Otherwise, fill up on a lot of fruits, veggies, grains, and other healthful foods. Don't be afraid to enjoy ice cream and other snacks—the key is simply to eat everything, including junk food, in moderation. Also, be sure to get out and get plenty of exercise, like riding your bike, playing sports, and walking. Follow these simple steps and you're more likely to stay at a weight you're happy with for life, instead of repeatedly losing and gaining weight like most dieters do.

Nutrition

Keep It Simple!

Some girls get obsessed about eating "just right." Remember, these are just guidelines. Some days you'll eat better or less healthy than others. Just aim to eat healthful foods when you can and you'll be A-okay!

Check It Out!

American Dietetic Association
216 West Jackson Boulevard
Chicago, Illinois 60606-6995
Phone: (312) 899-0040
Web site: www.eatright.org (includes a link for finding a registered dietitian)

Posture

Stand Tall and Proud

Posture is all about how you hold yourself. Good posture means standing and sitting straight so your head, neck, and back are in line with each other. It's holding your chest high, keeping your head up, and avoiding poor posture mistakes like slumping, slouching, and hunching forward. Good posture not only makes you look better, it's also better for you. It helps your bones grow in proper alignment and even improves your mood. Here's what you need to know about standing straight as you grow taller.

Q. I'm really tall and sometimes find myself scrunching over so I don't stand out so much. Is this as bad for me as my mom says it is?

A. Since girls usually go through their growth spurt before boys, they often find themselves towering over their classmates, especially the boys, at early ages—and feeling pretty self-conscious about it. But don't! Being tall is something you'll appreciate as you grow older—that's why so many women wear high heels!

As far as it being bad for you, sorry to say your mom's right. Slumping postures can lead to permanently rounded shoulders, making you looked hunched over even when you want to stand tall. What's more, having proper posture now helps protect you from problems like back pain and arthritis later in life.

Q. How can I tell if I'm standing "right"?

A. When you're standing with proper posture, you look like you have an imaginary string pulling the top of your head toward the sky. Your neck is long, your chin is level and slightly back, you have a slight arch in your lower back, and your chest is lifted so your shoulders naturally fall back. The best way to achieve this: Stand with your back against a wall. Try to touch your entire back to the wall, especially your upper back and shoulder blades. Your low back (where the arch is) won't touch the wall, but most of the rest of it will. Feel how your chest is open and your spine is nice and straight? That's how you should feel when you're standing and walking. Maintaining that fabulous posture is simply a matter of training your muscles to hold you in that position.

"I'm really tall for my age. But I stand straight because it looks better than slumping over."

Julie, 11

Q. My parents say not to slouch when I sit. How am I supposed to sit?

A. Believe it or not, you should sit the same way you stand: spine straight, shoulders back, head high. What we tend to do instead is slouch over forward, like when you're hunkered over your homework at night. Or we slump back, rounding our lower backs, like when you're chilling out on the sofa watching your favorite video. To avoid too much slouching and slumping, try to choose a chair with a backrest that helps you sit up straight. When you're working at a desk, try to move your chair close enough to your desk so that you don't have to lean way over to do your work.

Q. What other kinds of things can I do to improve my posture?

A. Again, your posture is all about how you hold yourself, and *lots* of stuff can affect whether you're standing tall or slouching. Here are some of the top posture helpers:

- **Move that body.** Strong, flexible, balanced muscles help you keep your back straight no matter what you're doing. That means getting off your butt and moving that body of yours as much as you can! Run, swim, ride your bike, Rollerblade, swing from tree limbs—whatever you love to do. Just do it.

- **Junk the junk.** It's tough to stand tall when you've got an achy belly from too much greasy junk food. Reach for those healthful, won't-weigh-you-down fruits, veggies, and whole grains whenever possible.

- **Think happy thoughts.** Take a look in the mirror sometime when you're feeling blue. What do you see? Rounded back, shoulders sloped forward—you probably look an inch, maybe two or three, shorter. Then sneak a peek at yourself when you've just aced a test. You're standing so stall, you've probably *gained* an inch or two. The motto: Stay positive, and your posture will look positive.

- **Pull that pack.** A thirty-pound, fully loaded backpack can be your back's worst nightmare, especially if you have the habit of slinging it over just one shoulder, causing your spine to curve and the weighed-down shoulder to slump. Either use both straps to evenly distribute the weight or, even better, use a travel-type pack, with wheels and a handle. That way you can pull it to the bus stop instead of carrying it on your back.

- **Wear smart shoes.** Heels are fun once in a while. But wearing them day in and day out can throw your posture way out of whack. Stick to cool, flat-soled sporty shoes, like cute slip-on sneakers, that support your feet *and* help improve your posture.

Stuck in a Slump?

Most of the time, poor posture is just from habit, the result of simply not standing or sitting straight. Sometimes, however, a girl (or a boy) *can't* stand straight now matter how hard she (or he) tries. This is usually a sign of a skeletal problem (see Caution: Dangerous Curves Ahead!, page 236). If you find that you can't straighten your spine and hold your shoulders level and back, talk to your parents about getting a checkup with a doctor. Most of these problems can be fixed, so you'll stand, sit, look, and *feel* better.

Check It Out!

Web site: www.spineuniverse.com (all you ever wanted to know about sitting, standing, moving, even sleeping with good posture)

Shaving & Hair Removal

The Hair-Grazing Facts for Shedding Unwanted Fuzz

Now that you've sprouted body hair, you're likely wondering what to do about it. Some girls aren't bugged by a little extra fuzz on their legs and underarms, so they go for the "natural" look and let the hair be. Others totally hate it and try to rid themselves of every stray strand. If you're bummed out about unwanted body hair, first get your parents' okay to remove it, then pick the best removal method for you. Here are the answers you need to lose the hair you don't want.

Q. What's the best way to get rid of body hair?

A. Hair removal is a multibillion-dollar industry in America, so you have many, many choices available to you, including razors, creams, and waxes. Which one you choose depends on the location of the hair, your hair type, your skin type, and your personal preference. Here are the pros and cons of the most common methods:

- **Razor shaving.** Cutting hair at the surface of the skin with a blade.

  Pros: Shaving is the quickest, cheapest, and probably the easiest way to shed unwanted hair—especially on the legs and underarms. It doesn't hurt (unless you nick your skin with the blade), and you can do it almost anytime, anywhere.

  Cons: Hair regrows quickly, in a few days, and feels stubbly. It can also cause irritating red bumps along your bikini line and elsewhere if you have sensitive skin or coarse hair.

  Tips: Use a disposable, sensitive-skin razor, and replace it after every five to seven shaves. Use a shaving gel, which helps the razor slide better on your skin. Shave against the direction of hair growth (upward on your legs, downward on your underarms) for the closest shave. Shaving in the same direction as hair growth is less irritating to very sensitive skin, but it will leave a little stubble. Soaking in a warm bath for a few minutes before shaving makes the hair softer so you're less likely to get razor burn. Moisturize your legs afterward.

"I shave my legs, like, every other day. If it's summer, then I shave them every day."

Tara, 13

- **Electric shaving/buzzing.** Removing hair at the surface of skin with an electric razor.

  Pros: You can do it outside the shower, it's quick and easy, and you can do it anytime, anywhere.

Cons: The shave from an electric razor can feel less smooth and close than a blade razor. Electric razors are much more expensive, and they're noisier to use. Hair grows back in a day or two.

Tips: Putting a little baby powder on your skin before shaving helps the razor glide more smoothly and gives you a better shave. Change the blade as recommended—usually every six months.

- **Creams.** You can use chemical creams, called depilatories (duh•PILL•uh•tor•ees), to dissolve the hair just below the surface of the skin. You smear them on, let them "work" for a few minutes, then wipe them and the unwanted hair away.

Pros: Your skin is smoother, and the results last longer. Hair can take a couple weeks to a month to grow back. The products are pretty cheap, and you can do it yourself in a few minutes.

Cons: Harsh chemicals in the creams can burn or irritate some skin types. They're also messy and smell pretty nasty. You shouldn't use them for underarm hair.

Tips: Always follow the directions on the label. Some creams are made especially for your face, while others are strong enough for your bikini line. Always test a small patch of skin first to be sure you won't have a bad reaction.

- **Waxing.** This involves pouring wax over your skin, letting it harden around the hair, then pulling the hair out by the root.

Pros: It lasts a month or more, and the result is very smooth, especially around the bikini line.

Cons: Ouch!! Pulling hair out by the roots is as painful as it sounds. You have to let hair grow in a quarter of an inch before you can wax again, which means living with lots of stubble. You can't wax your underarms. Skin can be pink and irritated immediately after waxing.

Tips: Although you can buy do-it-yourself home waxing kits, it is safer and you'll get better results letting a professional do it at a beauty salon. It's more expensive—anywhere from $15 to $50 a leg—but it's worth it if waxing is what you want.

- **Tweezing.** Using a tweezers to pluck out hair by the root, one by one.

  Pros: It's cheap and relatively easy to do. If you get the hair by the root, it can take a few weeks before you have to pluck again.

  Cons: B-O-R-I-N-G. Yanking out hair by hair is time consuming and somewhat painful. And it's totally impractical for big stuff like legs.

  Tips: Tweezing is best for stray hairs around eyebrows, nipples, and the belly. For best results, pluck hair right after you shower or bathe when your pores are more open and the hairs are soft.

- **Electrolysis.** Using an electric current to kill the hair at the root.

  Pros: Once the root is zapped, it's gone for good, so you get permanent removal.

  Cons: It hurts. It's expensive. And it can take a long time. Removing a mustache, for instance, would take weekly visits for a few months and cost several hundred dollars. You could put a down payment on a car for what it would cost to do your legs.

  Tips: Only a trained professional can perform electrolysis. Ask your doctor for a recommendation. Get references, so you can call other people who have had the procedure done by the professional you're considering before scheduling an appointment.

- **Lasering.** Zapping hair follicles with a laser to destroy the follicle and produce near-permanent hair removal.

Pros: Lasering is good for people with dark hair and fair skin. It works well for the bikini line, underarms, and lower legs. It produces long-term hair removal.

Cons: It's very expensive. Several treatments are needed for permanent reduction in hair growth.

Tips: Same as electrolysis—only a trained professional can do it, and you should always check references before making an appointment.

- **Bleaching.** Chemically lightening hair so it's less noticeable.

Pros: Since you're not removing the skin, you don't have to worry about stubble. It's relatively painless and easy to do. Results can last about a month.

Cons: The chemicals can irritate some skin types. It's not good for darker skin complexions, since light hair stands out more, and it's not practical for legs or underarms.

Tips: Bleaching is best for facial hair on light skin. Be sure you buy special bleaching products designed for use on the skin. Never use laundry or hair bleach. Always test a small patch in a less visible area first to be sure you don't have a bad reaction.

"I usually shave my legs about once or twice a week. During school vacations, I sometimes shave them more."

Liz, 13

Q. Does shaving hair make it grow back thicker and darker?

A. Nope. It just looks that way. Unshaved, your hair is long and tapers at the end, giving it a more fine appearance. Once shaven, you cut off that tapered portion, so the hair pokes back out of the skin with a blunt, thicker end. That's why it looks coarser and darker.

Q. What can I do about the hair on my upper lip?

A. Facial depilatories, like Nair for the face, are good for shedding fine moustaches and facial hair. You can also try bleaching it, but that works best on fairer complexions because the bleach also lightens the skin a little, which can be pretty noticeable on darker skin.

Q. Why do I get these irritating bumps around my bikini area when I shave?

A. The bumps are ingrown hairs. The hair around your pubic region is thicker and curlier than the hair on the rest of your legs. What happens is that as the hair starts growing back, the tip of it curls right back toward your body and pierces the skin. These spots can become infected and irritated. If this happens, free the free end from the skin. But don't pluck the hair—that can cause scarring. If you're prone to ingrown hairs in this area, try waxing or using a depilatory in those areas rather than shaving, since those methods don't cut hair into a sharp point like shaving does.

When It's More Than Just Fuzz . . .

A little increase in facial hair is normal around puberty. But a sudden increase in facial hair can be a symptom of a more serious condition. So if noticeable facial hair doesn't run in your family or if it seemed to come on overnight, ask your mom or dad to make an appointment with your doctor just to be sure everything's okay.

Shaving & Hair Removal

Check It Out!

American Academy of Dermatology (AAD)
930 North Meacham Road
P.O. Box 4014
Schaumburg, Illinois 60168-4014
Phone: (847) 330-0230
Web site: www.aad.org (has a special "Kid's Connection" link
for preteens and adolescents)

Shaving & Hair Removal

Sleep

The Rest You Need to Recharge

Though we tend to take it for granted, sleep is every bit as important as food and water for how healthy we grow and how good we feel. Skimp on your shut-eye and your brain stops working, your immunity against sickness plunges, your mood sinks like a stone, and you probably won't look very rosy either. In fact, like starvation (depriving yourself of food), you can actually die from total sleep deprivation! Growing girls especially need plenty of ZZZZs, since all those changes you're going through take a lot of energy, and your body needs the downtime to recharge. Here's the scoop on getting enough sleep.

"I go to bed between 9:00 and 10:00 P.M. and wake up between 6:00 and 8:00 A.M. I get plenty of sleep!"

Britany, 11

Q. How much sleep do I need each night?

A. Preteen girls need between nine and eleven hours of sleep each night. That's a little bit more than your parents need, which is why they may stay up a little later than you. But remember,

226

you're going through one of the biggest growth spurts of your life, and that means you need lots of rest!

Q. Sometimes I just lie in bed and toss and turn. Why can't I just fall right to sleep?

A. Everyone has a bout of "insomnia," or not being able to sleep, once in a while. One common cause is too much stimulation before bedtime—from television or the computer or a video game or any other activity that leaves you wide-eyed when you lie down. Try the following tips to help you fall asleep faster:

- **Be consistent about bedtime.** Your body is a creature of habit. It works best if you go to bed and wake up about the same time every day. So if you sleep in 'til noon on Sunday, you're bound to have trouble going to sleep at 9:00 or 10:00 P.M. and waking up early on Monday. Try to get up within an hour or so of the same time every morning, even on weekends.

- **Set a wind-down time.** Studies show that watching television is a big sleep disturber. So are video games and even just playing around on the computer. The problem is all these activities stimulate your brain, and your brain doesn't just automatically shut down when you push the power button off. Ideally, you need about one-half hour to an hour of quiet time before you hit the hay so your body can wind down naturally. The best stuff to do: Listen to music, write in your journal, read. Add some restful activity into your nightly routine of washing your face and brushing your teeth and you're almost sure to sleep more soundly.

- **Be active during the day.** A tired body is a sleepy body. Regular exercise wears you out, so you want to sleep. Plus, physical activity is a great way to blow off stress that can keep you up at night. Just don't run around too close to bedtime or you could be too wound up to feel tired.

- **Skip the soda.** Caffeine is a stimulating chemical that works wonders in keeping your body awake. That's why millions

Sleep

of adults drink coffee—which is loaded with caffeine—
to wake up every day. Well, a lot of the sodas you drink,
especially colas, Mountain Dew, and Dr. Pepper, contain
caffeine, too. And if you drink them too late in the day, like
after dinnertime, you could find yourself staring at the ceil-
ing when you want to be asleep. Other foods that contain
caffeine: tea, chocolate (a cup of warm, steamy cocoa is
probably not the right bedtime choice after all), and anything with coffee in it, like coffee ice cream.

- **Eat lightly.** A nighttime snack of cookies and milk can be
  a perfect way to wind down and to stop a rumbling
  tummy from keeping you awake. But don't eat too much.
  A too-full belly can have the opposite affect.

- **Practice "progressive relaxation."** If you're lying in bed
  feeling all jazzed up from the day, practice some progressive relaxation to wind your body down. Start with your
  toes. Concentrate on stretching them out and relaxing
  them. Work your way up through your legs, tummy, back,
  and arms, all the way up to your face. By the time you
  reach the top of your head you should feel more relaxed.

- **Talk to someone.** Sometimes we have trouble sleeping because we have worried minds. If stress at school or anxiety
  at home is following you into bed and keeping you up,
  you need to talk to an adult you trust. Taking a load off
  your mind will help you get more rest at night.

Q. I'm so afraid of the dark, sometimes I
feel like I'm up all night. What can I do?

A. Get some ghostbusters, girl! Being afraid of the dark is very,
very common. When everything is dark and quiet, ordinary objects in your room and in the house look and sound different,
which can creep out even the bravest girl. Talk to your parents
about getting a nightlight, so you can see that there's nothing in
your room that's going to hurt you. Hear funny noises? Your
mom and dad can probably explain that the knocking you hear

is the water heater, not witches. Is the silence scary? Try playing some soft background noise like a CD of ocean sounds or even just running a fan to fill the air and lull you to sleep. With a little help, you can slay whatever nighttime dragons are spooking you and get some shut eye once and for all.

"I usually go to bed around 9:00 P.M. and get up around 7:30 in the morning. I feel like I get plenty of sleep."

Samantha, 9

Q. I'm eleven years old and still sometimes wet my bed. I'm so embarrassed that I never go to sleepovers. Will it ever stop?

A. It's understandable that you feel embarrassed. But what you have is a medical condition called *enuresis* that you shouldn't feel ashamed about. A lot of different things, from heredity (meaning it runs in the family) to different medical conditions, can cause you to pee in your bed at night, even at age eleven. But that doesn't mean you have to stay away from slumber parties forever. Talk to your parents about working with your doctor to help solve your problem. She will be able to diagnose any medical conditions that could be causing it, and she'll also be able to offer solutions, ranging from changes in your bedtime routine to medications to help you stay dry through the night. Rest assured, you're not alone in your bed-wetting woes, and it's something that can be cured.

Q. I have scary dreams that wake me up in the middle of the night. How can I make myself have nice dreams?

A. There's no surefire way to keep those creepy nightmares at bay. Your brain uses sleep time to clean out its closets and work through issues you may have encountered during the day. Sometimes the result is a bad dream, which is totally normal, even though it's troubling at the time. That said, if you're getting jolted awake by nasty nightmares every night, it could be a sign that something is really bothering you. Did you watch a movie that upset you? Was there a scary story in the newspaper? Is something going on at school? Think about the stuff that might be bothering you and talk to your parents or a guidance counselor about it. Once you get rid of the scary daytime mind clutter, it'll be less likely to come back and haunt you at night.

Sleepiness Can Be a Sickness

A lot of kids, 20 to 30 percent, have some sort of sleep trouble at some time or other. But if you frequently have trouble waking up in the morning, feel tired during the day, fall asleep in school, and feel cranky and have trouble concentrating on your class work, it's time to see a doctor. Also, have your parents check to see if you snore a lot at night. If you do, your mom should schedule an appointment for you to see your doctor—you could have a sleep condition that's robbing you of your rest. Your doctor can help.

Check It Out!

National Sleep Foundation
1522 K Street N.W., Suite 500
Washington, D.C. 20005
Phone: (202) 347-3471
Web site: www.sleepfoundation.org

Sleep

Strong Bones

The Frame for Your Beautiful Body

Though you can't see them all, you have more than 200 bones in your body that make up your skeleton. Without bones, there's not much you could do except lie there on the floor like a blob of pudding. Your muscles pull on your bones to help you run, jump, play, even just sit still in a chair. Right now, your bones are in their prime forming years, and those bones are going to have to last for the rest of your life—maybe more than a hundred years! That's why it's very, very important to take good care of them now, so they grow as healthy and strong as they can be. Here's the inside scoop on getting a super skeleton.

Q. How long will my bones continue to grow?

A. As you read this your bones are probably still getting longer. Bones go through a big growth spurt before you get your first period, then once you start menstruating, they continue to grow at a slower rate for about two more years. So if it seems like you're growing like a weed right now, it's because you are!

Even after your bones are finished getting as long as they're going to get, they're still not done growing. Your bones continue to get thicker and denser—a very important part of their development—through your mid-twenties, even up until you're about thirty years old. Sometime after your bones reach maximum density, they actually start getting a little weaker, and you continue losing little bits of bone mass as you age. That's why you want to do everything you can to make that skeleton as strong as you can while it's still growing, so it's still plenty strong later in life.

Q. Do all my bones grow?

A. To some extent, yes. But some definitely grow more than others. When you're a baby, your head actually accounts for about a quarter of your length. If your head were to continue to grow so it was a quarter of your height, you'd look like an alien! During puberty, you'll notice that your hips and legs seem to grow the most. Your pelvic bones (which are your hips) become broader, and your femurs (the thigh bones) become longer. Of course, other bones grow, too. Your arms get longer, your shoulders broaden, and your hands and feet get bigger. Even your face bones grow. Your face becomes longer— your chin juts out, your forehead becomes higher and wider, your nose lengthens, and your cheekbones become more prominent. That's why if you line up school pictures of yourself from kindergarten through your current grade, you'll look way different every year!

"I'm very active, but I've never broken a bone."

Liz, 13

Q. What are growing pains?

A. If your legs have ever felt cramped or tired and achy in the afternoon or evening (and you haven't been outside sprinting), you may have felt growing pains. Sometimes bones grow faster than the muscles they're attached to. The result is muscle pain, usually behind the knee, in the thighs, and along the shins, though you can feel growing pains almost anywhere, including your arms, shoulders, back, and ankles. Remember how you grow most quickly right before you get your first period? Well, it's probably no coincidence that growing pains are most common between the ages of ten and eleven, right around the time when most girls' bodies are getting ready to begin menstruating.

Growing pains are uncomfortable, but they don't last long, and you often can make them feel better by having one of your parents rub the sore area or by taking a pain reliever (always ask your parents first) if the pain is keeping you from sleeping. If the pain is really bad or keeps happening night after night, you should probably talk to your doctor just to make sure everything else is okay.

Q. What can I do to help my bones get strong?

A. The two most important things you can do for healthy, strong bones are eat right and exercise. Your bones are made out of calcium, a mineral that is found in milk and dairy foods like yogurt and cheese as well as in leafy green veggies like broccoli and spinach. Obviously, since your bones are made from calcium, you need *plenty* of calcium in your diet to help them grow. Too many girls steer clear of milk, because they're afraid it's "fattening." Nothing could be further from the truth. A glass of skim milk has no more calories—sometimes fewer—than a glass of iced tea or soda, and it's so much better for you. So shoot for three glasses a day—one with every meal—and reach for yogurt, cheese, and other calcium-filled snacks frequently, too. If you don't like milk, look for calcium-fortified orange juice (it'll say so right on the label).

Hand in hand with eating the right stuff is moving your body. Exercise helps the calcium you eat become part of your bones. So get out and play as much as you can. Great bone-building activities include jumping rope, shooting baskets, walking, and any sport that has you running around. The worst thing you can do for your bones is spend a lot of time sitting in front of the television or the computer.

When you're older, like in your mid to late teens and definitely in your twenties and beyond, you'll also want to do some strength training. Strength training is any activity that makes your muscles strong, like lifting weights and doing calisthenics like pushups. Strength training isn't good for your bones while they're still getting longer, which is why you shouldn't do it until you're in your teens, but it's great for making bones thick and strong. It makes your muscles look nice, too.

Q. What kind of stuff is bad for my bones?

A. Again, sitting around watching television or using the computer for hours on end is bad news for your bones because they don't get any use. Smoking is also terrible for your bones, as it actually sucks calcium out of them! When you look at pictures of smoker's bones, they look like Swiss cheese—they have big holes in them. Eating a diet filled with too much junk food and not much healthful, calcium-filled foods hurts your bones by not giving them what they need to grow. Some experts think that drinking too much soda also can lead to weak bones. And finally, maybe one of the worst things for young, developing bones is dieting. Girls who diet don't get enough of the important nutrients their bones need to grow. What's more, girls who diet too much, especially if they combine dieting with excessive exercise (like the kind serious athletes do), can stop having their periods. This is the worst thing that can happen to your bones, and they can literally get brittle and never fully recover. So a healthy diet and exercise is definitely the key.

Q. I got a stress fracture last summer at soccer camp. What causes that?

A. Sounds like you overdid it. Since your bones are still developing, they're not yet able to handle all the stresses that adult bones can take, like kicking a ball over and over and over and over. Sometimes the bones will develop a fine crack, or a stress fracture, from that kind of repetitive stress. Stress fractures don't happen to everyone, but they can happen to quite a few young athletes. You don't need to stop playing soccer, but it's a good idea to mix up your activities, especially while your bones are still growing. Try swimming, basketball, bicycling, and all the other sports and activities life has to offer. You might find something else you really love, and you'll be giving your developing bones the right kind of break.

"I worry about breaking bones because my mom broke her arm and it hurt for months and never healed right."

Chris, 13

Q. My grandmother has osteoporosis. Does that mean I'll get it, too?

A. Not necessarily, although you do want to be good to those bones of yours because osteoporosis can run in families. When someone has osteoporosis, it means their bones are extremely brittle and thin, and they can fracture their hips, wrists, legs, and spine with the slightest bumps or falls. If you've ever seen an older woman who is stooped over and has a rounded back, that's a sign of osteoporosis. What happens is the vertebrae (the bones in the spine) are so weak, they actually compress, so she couldn't straighten up if she tried. Osteoporosis can make it hard to live and enjoy life—another big reason to work on keeping those bones strong every day.

Caution: Dangerous Curves Ahead!

Most of the time, your bones grow nice and straight without any outside assistance. Sometimes, however, bones, particularly those in your spine, don't grow as straight as they should and need help. When your spine curves to one side or the other, it's called scoliosis. It may make one hip or shoulder noticeably higher than the other. Or, if it's a very slight curve, you may not see anything different when you look in the mirror. Though both boys and girls can have it, scoliosis tends more often to progress, or get worse, in girls. Because this condition can cause problems as you grow, it's important to get tested during your prime growing years—between the ages of nine and fifteen. The good news is that even if the doctor or nurse testing you finds a slight curve in your spine, there's a good chance that it won't get any worse and won't need any treatment. If it does start curving more, most cases of scoliosis can be treated with a back brace that holds your spine stable and straight while you grow. No, it's not much fun to wear a brace, but there are new braces now that are thinner and more flexible, so it's less of a drag. In very few cases, kids need surgery to fix their scoliosis. The bottom line is just to get screened and keep an eye on a spinal curve, if you have one, so you can get it fixed and get on with your life.

Check It Out!

American Academy of Orthopaedic Surgeons
6300 North River Road
Rosemont, Illinois 60018-4262
Phone: (800) 346-AAOS (2267)
Web site: www.aaos.org

Sunshine

Fun—and Safety—in the Sun

No question, the sun rocks. Long summer days at the beach and on the boardwalk and playing outside in the warmth of the sun's rays are some of life's most awesome pleasures. And you actually *need* some time in the sun to grow up healthy! But as you know, the sun's rays are mighty strong and can be dangerous if you're not careful. Here's the scoop on having safe fun in the sun.

"Where I live, it's sunny during the summer and spring but the rest of the year it usually isn't. I use sunscreen when I go to the beach or pool and when I'm at camp or on vacation."

Liz, 13

Q. I always hear I need to protect myself from the sun. Then I hear the sun is good for me. Which is it—good or bad?

A. Like a lot of stuff in life, the sun is good for you in small doses. In fact, you need sun exposure to be healthy. When sunshine hits your skin, it triggers a chemical reaction that makes vitamin D—an essential nutrient you need to build bones. Without sunshine, your bones would literally turn so soft your legs would bow from trying to hold you upright. So *some* time out in the sun is a must. Unfortunately, you can always get too much of a good thing—sunshine included. Too much time in the sun—*especially without the proper protection*—also can cause other troubling conditions, like burns; wrinkles; brown spots; and, worst of all, cancer.

Yeah, wrinkles and cancer don't sound to you like stuff you need to worry about when you're eleven, but they actually are. See, *now* is the time when those problems start. According to the Skin Cancer Foundation, 80 percent of our lifetime sun exposure happens *before* we reach the age of eighteen—like right now for you. So once you reach the age where you might start worrying about those bad things, the damage is done.

Q. How does the sun burn your skin?

A. Sunlight hits the skin with two kinds of ultraviolet rays (types of light): UVA and UVB. UVB rays are high-powered stuff. When they're absorbed by the surface of the skin, they cause a burn. To try to soothe the fire, your body pumps blood and healing cells to the surface of the skin, which causes that bright red appearance. UVA rays are also strong, but in a different way. They penetrate below the skin's surface and cause damage like wrinkles later in life.

Q. Will sunscreen protect me?

A. It sure helps! But it's important that you use the right kind and apply it often. When chilling outdoors, look for a sunscreen that offers "broad spectrum" protection—that means it protects against both UVA and UVB radiation. It should have a sun protection factor (SPF) rating of at least 15. Make sure it's waterproof, if you plan on swimming or will be sweating a lot. If you're going to be kicking it on the beach all day, especially between 10:00 A.M. and 4:00 P.M. when the sun is at its strongest, you should use a "sunblock" that contains titanium dioxide or zinc oxide because the water and sand make the sun's rays even stronger. Don't forget to put it around your eyes, your ears, and your lips. And remember, the sun's rays penetrate your skin even on cloudy days, so it's a good idea to find a moisturizer with SPF protection and use it even when you think you don't need it. For max protection, apply sunscreen at least twenty minutes before you head out the door to give it time to soak in. Reapply it every two hours—more frequently if you're going in and out of the water. The best way to make sure you're always protected is to throw a bottle of sunscreen in your backpack and take it with you wherever you go. If you have fair skin, burn easily, or plan to be out in the sun all day long, you should definitely bring some clothing protection as well as sunscreen. Covering up with a broad-brimmed hat to shade your face and a T-shirt can help you from getting fried after a long day in the sun.

"I usually only wear sunscreen
if I'm going to be in the sun all day because
I only tan and usually don't get sunburned."

Tara, 13

Q. I know it's bad for me, but I love looking tan. Isn't there anything I can do?

A. There's really no safe way to tan. A suntan is what happens when you repeatedly injure your skin with exposure to the sun's rays. To protect itself, your skin produces more of a pigment called melanin. But over time, tanning changes the texture of your skin, causing wrinkles, spots, and a leathery feeling. You'll likely get a little bit of color even if you use sunscreens. But if that's not enough and you must have the sunbronzed look for summer, try a fake bake. The new self-tanners don't turn you freak orange like the old ones did. Products like Coppertone Endless Summer Sunless Tanning Lotion run about ten bucks and leave your skin safe and "sun-kissed." Of course, the trick is applying the stuff evenly, so you might want to recruit a pal to help.

Soothe That Sun-Scorched Skin

So you blew it, and stayed out in the sun too long. Now your skin is screaming and you look like a tasty Red Lobster dish. Soothe your burn by applying a cream that has aloe vera in it, a burn-calming substance that comes from aloe plants. You can buy aloe-containing burn lotions at the drug store. Or rub yourself down with some water mixed with white vinegar. You can also take an over-the-counter pain reliever like ibuprofen (Advil) to help ease the inflammation and pain. And finally, if you end up getting blisters, dab some antibiotic healing ointment like polysporin on the sore spots to keep them from getting infected.

Check It Out!

Skin Cancer Foundation
Box 561, Department SA
New York, New York 10156
Web site: www.skincancer.org (a lot of sun protection info for everyone)

Sunshine

Tattoos & Piercings

Permanent Decorations

You can hardly watch a basketball game or a music awards show without seeing body art of all kinds. From thick, black-ink armbands to skinny, silver eyebrow hoops, all kinds of celebrities, from actors to athletes, are sporting tattoos and body piercings of all kinds these days. Though it's been in fashion for just the last few years, it's hardly anything new. Thousands of years ago, ancient Egyptians, Mayans, and Romans—just to name a few—pierced, inked, and scarred their bodies, often as part of spiritual rituals or as symbols of strength and fertility. Though expressing yourself though body art sounds fun and exciting, it's also painful and *permanent,* and it could lead to serious complications—if not serious regrets—a few years later when you change your mind! Here are the answers you need about body art.

Q. How do they get tattoos on your skin?

A. A tattoo is created with a special electric instrument that uses needles to inject ink into the top layers of your skin. Because the ink actually goes several layers into your skin it doesn't rub off like it does when you write on your skin with a pen.

"I think that it's stupid to get a tattoo because it lasts forever and you might not always want it. Then the only way to get rid of it is through really expensive surgery. I have my ears pierced and I might possibly pierce some other part of my body when I'm older, but probably not."

Liz, 13

Q. Can I get a tattoo removed if I don't like it?

A. Maybe. But you definitely shouldn't count on it. Special doctors can use lasers to vaporize the pigment and eventually blast away the tattoo. But it takes many treatments; some colors are harder to get rid of than others; it hurts a whole lot; and the multiple treatments it requires can cost hundreds, if not thousands, of dollars to get the job done. Even if you do succeed in obliterating the unwanted butterfly on your arm, you may end up with a permanently discolored spot where the tattoo once was.

Concern about changing your mind is one of the biggest reasons to skip getting a tattoo. Studies show that a whole lot of men and women regret getting the tattoos they have. Think you'll never grow to hate a tattoo you get as a teen? Go back and look at pictures of yourself with hairstyles or clothes you used to love but that you now think look silly or out of date. Your taste in tattoos is no different from hairstyles, clothes, or music. It changes as you grow. So it's really, really important to be 100 percent sure it's something you want to live with forever.

A better idea: Opt for temporary tattoos. You can get great designs that stick on and last for a few weeks before washing off. There are even rhinestone stick-on tattoos, so you can put a red sparkly heart on your shoulder for a special event, then take it off when you're tired of it.

Q. How much do tattoos cost?

A. Depends on where you get them done, how big they are, and how many colors are involved. Very small tattoos can be fifty to a hundred dollars. Larger ink art can cost thousands.

Q. Are tattoos safe?

A. They can be. They can also be very unsafe. Never, ever, ever let a friend or someone who is not a professional tattooist with professional sterilization equipment put any ink on you, period. Dirty or infected tattooing (and piercing) equipment and needles can spread potentially fatal diseases and infections, like hepatitis and even HIV (the virus that causes AIDS). Remember, you can't see the infection-causing germs, so even if a needle looks clean, that doesn't mean it's safe.

If you ever do decide to get a tattoo and your parents agree (in many states, your parents need to sign a form of consent if you're under the age of 18), be sure the professional who applies the tattoo has an autoclave or heat sterilization machine to sterilize the tattoo gun between customers. Ink should be poured into plastic cups and thrown out after every tattoo. You should get fresh, sterile needles that are thrown out after use. And the tattooist should wear gloves at all times. Ask a lot of questions about safety. A good tattooist will be happy to answer them. If you don't get the answers you're looking for, go somewhere else.

Unfortunately, even if a tattooist does everything right, there's still a chance for infection. The tattooist will give detailed directions for caring for the tattoo until it heals, which includes washing it and applying special antibiotic ointments. It's important to follow these directions carefully. And finally, some people are allergic to tattoo dye. If that happens, your body will reject the tattoo no matter what you do.

Tattoos & Piercings

Q. Do tattoos hurt?

A. You bet! You're getting injected with needles thousands of times. It hurts a lot.

Q. I want to get my ears pierced, but my mom says I'm too young. How old do you have to be?

A. There's no magical age for getting your ears pierced —many states have rules about piercing if you are under the age of 18 and usually require a parent's consent. So it really is up to your parents as to when you're "old enough" to get your ears pierced. She might be concerned about infections, since you have to pay special attention to cleaning your piercings until they heal. Or maybe she wants your ear piercing to mark a special time in your life. Some mothers like their daughters to wait until they get their first period or until they are 13, so it becomes a celebration of becoming a young woman. Talk to your mom about the reasons she wants you to wait and find out when she thinks is the right time for you to get earrings. Then you'll have a time to look forward to. In the meantime, do your best to be patient. Once your ears are pierced, they'll be pierced for life, and this little wait won't seem like such a big deal.

"I have my ears pierced. I like temporary tattoos. But if they're real, I don't like them."

Kortni, 10

Q. Is it safe to get other places besides your earlobes pierced?

A. Sometimes. But there's no doubt that some sites are more prone to infections than others. While your ears are pretty safe for piercing, other areas of the body, like your navel, nipples, and genitals (yep, some people even get *that* area pierced) are

Tattoos & Piercings

generally covered by clothes and don't have much air circulation. These areas are more prone to becoming irritated by the rubbing of your clothes and infected by bacteria and sweat. And nipple piercings may damage some of your milk-producing ducts, which can cause problems if you want to breastfeed a baby when you're an adult.

Other problems, including serious infections and even the transmission of diseases like HIV, can occur if you get pierced with a dirty needle. It's very important to get any piercing done in a clean, professional establishment. The person doing the piercing should wear gloves, and the equipment should always be sterilized. Any jewelry in a newly pierced hole should be stainless steel, 14-karat gold, niobium, titanium, or platinum to avoid infections or allergic reactions. Your piercer should use a hand tool rather than a piercing gun, since a piercing gun cannot be sterilized properly. Once you're pierced, the piercer should give you detailed advice about taking care of the pierced site including how to clean it. Be sure to follow those directions carefully.

Q. How long does it take for a belly button ring to heal?

A. Anywhere from four months to a whole year. And even then, some people have trouble with their clothes irritating the piercing. Other piercing sites heal faster or slower, depending on where they are and what kind of tissue is pierced. Ear lobes heal pretty quickly, in about six to eight weeks. The cartilage that's higher up on the ear can take up to a year. Eyebrows take about six to eight weeks. Noses take two to four months; lips, two to three weeks; nipples, three to six months. And tongues actually heal in a pretty fast four weeks, though they swell pretty badly after the initial piercing and can cause problems like broken teeth and infection afterward.

Tattoos & Piercings

Watch for Infection

Tattoos and piercings leave a wound that needs to heal. Like any wound, these body decorations are at risk for getting infected. If you have a lot of redness and swelling at the site, let your mom or dad know right away. You may need to see a doctor to prevent a serious infection.

Check It Out!

American Academy of Dermatology (AAD)
930 North Meacham Road
Schaumburg, Illinois 60168-4014
Phone: (847) 330-0230
Web site: www.aad.org (they even have a cool link called
Kid's Connection for preteens and adolescents)

Tattoos & Piercings

Vitamins

The Vital Stuff You Need for Growing

Not to put more pressure on you or anything, but now is a really important time for your body. Your bones are growing thicker and longer, building up to a maximum density that has to last your whole life! You're growing taller, your body is developing, even your hair is growing fuller! So it's pretty important to eat right (see Nutrition, page 208) and get all the vitamins and minerals you need every day. Vitamins and minerals are natural chemicals and compounds found in the foods we eat. For hundreds of years, scientists have been identifying and studying these nutrients, figuring out what they do in our bodies and how much of them we need to be our strongest and healthiest. What they came up with is known today as "Daily Values" or "Recommended Intakes" (the amounts you see on food and supplement labels). Though some of the amounts are different depending on your age or if you're a girl or a boy or a man or a woman, many of them are the same no matter who you are. Here's what you need to know.

Q. What happens if I don't get enough nutrients?

A. If you get *way* below the recommended amounts—we're talking close to zero for months on end—*really* bad stuff can happen. Long ago, sailors used to come down with a disease called scurvy, which caused bleeding gums, pneumonia, and sometimes death, because they were out at sea without enough fresh fruits and veggies to give them vitamin C. Thousands of people died in the South around the time of World War I because an important B-vitamin named niacin was missing from their diets. And children in London and other cities used to come down with a crippling condition called rickets, which caused soft and deformed bones, because they weren't getting the vitamin D they needed. Today, a lot of the foods we eat every day are fortified with vitamins and minerals, so stuff like scurvy isn't a worry!

That said, though, it is easy to run a little low on important nutrients when you're eating on the run and grabbing foods that aren't very healthful. If really unhealthful eating becomes a habit, you can find yourself feeling draggy and irritable, and you may get sick more often. Your skin, hair, and nails can also end up looking dull and dry rather than healthy, strong, and shiny. So it's definitely smart to grab at least one well-rounded meal even on busy days.

One nutrient even kids who eat healthfully miss all too often: calcium. With soda and iced tea replacing milk at meals, experts at the National Institutes of Health say that nine out of ten girls and three out of four boys aged nine to seventeen do not get enough calcium. That can set you up for fragile bones later in life. Don't forget—your beverages count as part of a healthful diet, too. Shoot for three glasses of milk a day, one with every meal!

"I take a multivitamin every day."

Liz, 13

Q. How many vitamins and minerals do I need every day?

A. Generally speaking you should aim to get 100 percent of the Daily Value (DV) for all the essentials. The chart below (don't skip over it just because it's a chart—it tells you all the right foods to eat and how they help you. Just think, the next time you and your friends are eating, you can tell them how the food is helping them!) lists important vitamins and minerals, how much you need of each (you'll notice the measurements are different depending on the nutrient), and the foods you'll find them in. (There are even more minerals than what we've listed here, but these are the major ones to know about.)

The Growing Girl Vitamin Guide

Nutrient	DV	What It Does	Foods It's In
Vitamin A	5,000 International Units (IUs)	Protects eyes; promotes healthy tissues inside the nose, mouth, lungs, and digestive tract; prevents infection.	Milk, eggs, cheese, dark leafy green vegetables, orange and yellow fruits and vegetables
Vitamin B_1 (thiamin)	1.5 milli-grams (mg)	Helps turn food into energy.	Cereal, fish, whole grain breads, potatoes, eggs, poultry
Vitamin B_2 (riboflavin)	1.7 mg	Produces energy through-out your body.	Lean meats, cereal, whole grain breads, milk, spinach, poultry
Vitamin B_3 (niacin)	20 mg	Needed for growth; helps transform sugar and fatty acids to energy.	Lean meats, poultry, tuna, potatoes, cereal, corn, mushrooms, peas
Vitamin B_6 (pyridoxine)	2 mg	Helps your body use protein; boosts immune system.	Chick peas, peanut butter, poultry, sweet potatoes, cereal, spinach
Vitamin B_{12} (cobalamin)	6 micro-grams (mcg)	Necessary for producing red and white blood cells.	Milk, lean meats, poultry, yogurt, eggs
Folic acid	400 mcg	Keeps the nervous system healthy; needed for making DNA for new cells.	Spinach, beans, peas, lentils, broccoli, oranges, asparagus
Biotin	300 mcg	Helps metabolize food.	Nuts, peas, eggs, mushrooms, cauliflower

The Growing Girl Vitamin Guide (continued)

Nutrient	DV	What It Does	Foods It's In
Pantothenic acid	10 mg	Helps metabolize food.	Eggs, fish, broccoli, lean meats, nuts
Vitamin C	60 mg	Promotes healthy skin, cartilage, bones, and teeth; boosts immunity.	Citrus fruits, melons, berries, tomatoes, broccoli, bell peppers, leafy green vegetables
Vitamin D	400 IUs	Necessary for strong, healthy bones and teeth.	Sunshine, fortified milk, eggs, cereal
Vitamin E	30 IUs	Strengthens cells.	Nuts and seeds, vegetable oils, wheat germ
Vitamin K	80 mcg	Essential for healthy blood clotting (like when you cut yourself).	Broccoli, spinach, kale, other dark leafy green vegetables
Calcium	1,000 mg	Builds bones and teeth.	Milk, cheese, yogurt, fortified orange juice, salmon, dark leafy green vegetables
Copper	2 mg	Needed for healthy blood vessels.	Shellfish, especially oysters and lobster
Chromium	120 mcg	Helps your body use blood sugar.	Broccoli, grapefruit, turkey, fortified cereals
Iodine	150 mcg	Helps regulate metabolism.	The salt in foods contains all you need.
Iron	18 mg	Helps carry oxygen in the blood; needed for normal energy levels.	Lean meats, dried fruit, spinach, shellfish, beans, fortified cereals
Magnesium	400 mg	Helps build strong bones and healthy muscles and nerves.	Seafood, nuts, fortified cereals, whole grains, leafy green vegetables
Manganese	2 mg	Helps control chemical reactions in your body.	Whole grains, pineapple
Potassium	3,500 mg	Necessary for healthy muscles and nerves, especially if you play sports.	Bananas, potatoes, cantaloupe, figs, raisins, beans and peas, milk
Selenium	70 mcg	Protects cells from damage.	Onions, garlic, most fruits and vegetables
Zinc	15 mg	Builds immunity; helps wounds heal.	Lean meats, poultry, shellfish, fortified cereals

"I don't take vitamins."

Tara, 13

Q. Do I actually have to count how many milligrams of each nutrient I get every day?

A. No way! If you tried to count every milligram and microgram of all your vitamins and minerals every day, you would have little time left to go to school and do your homework! Instead, just check out the foods listed on the chart above and include them in your diet. If you follow the standard food pyramid (see page 172), you should be totally covered. If you're concerned, you can also take a daily multivitamin as nutrition "insurance." But remember your body gets more from real food than it does from a pill!

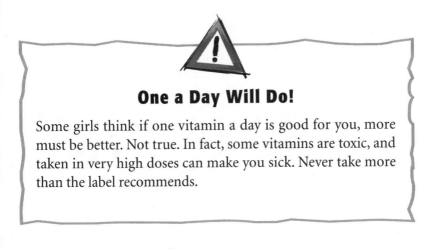

One a Day Will Do!

Some girls think if one vitamin a day is good for you, more must be better. Not true. In fact, some vitamins are toxic, and taken in very high doses can make you sick. Never take more than the label recommends.

Check It Out!

American Dietetic Association
216 West Jackson Boulevard
Chicago, Illinois 60606-6995
Phone: (312) 899-0040
Web site: www.eatright.org (includes link for finding a registered dietitian)

Panel of Advisers

Please meet our panel of experts. This esteemed group of people provided invaluable advice and generously lent their time, research, wisdom, and insight. Without them, this project would have been impossible.

Carolyn Jacob, M.D., is a dermatologist and cosmetic laser surgeon who works with young girls and clients of all ages at the Advanced Skin and Mohs Surgery Center in Skokie, Illinois. She also is a clinical instructor in dermatology at Northwestern University Medical School in Chicago.

Sharon Lehman, M.D., is chief of the division of ophthalmology in the department of surgery at Alfred I. duPont Hospital for Children in Wilmington, Delaware. She helps fix eye problems so kids can see better.

Iris Prager, Ph.D., is a health educator who specializes in reproductive and menstrual health and offers helpful information to women and teens at www.tampax.com and www.beinggirl.com. She also is the president of the American Association for Health Education.

Michele Innes, R.D., is a pediatric clinical dietitian at Alfred I. duPont Hospital for Children in Wilmington, Delaware. She has special training and expertise in the nutritional needs of infants, children, and teens, so she helps kids make smart food choices to keep them growing strong and healthy.

Michele Grodner, Ed.D., C.H.E.S., is a professor in the department of community health at William Paterson University in Wayne,

New Jersey. She is a specialist in nutrition and author of *Foundations and Clinical Applications of Nutrition: A Nursing Approach*, 2nd ed. St. Louis, MO: Mosby 2000). She has also authored *D.C. Superheroes Super Healthy Cookbook for Children* and she helped *Sesame Street* evaluate its health and nutrition segments.

Nadya Swedan, M.D., is a sports health specialist and author of *Women's Sports Medicine and Rehabilitation* (Human Kinetics 2001). She is in private practice with Manhattan Orthopedics and Sports Medicine, PC.

Barbara Ann Rich, D.D.S., is the national spokesperson for the Academy of General Dentistry, helping kids and people of all ages maintain bright smiles and healthy teeth and gums. She currently has a private dentistry practice in Cherry Hill, New Jersey.

Marla D. Kushner, D.O., F.S.A.M., is a clinical assistant professor at Midwestern University in Downer's Grove, Illinois. She has special training in adolescent medicine and addresses health questions of all kinds at www.askdoctormarla.com.

Meredith Barber, Psy.D., is an outpatient psychologist at The Renfrew Center, a women's health center that treats women for eating disorders, depression, and other mental health issues. She specializes in eating disorders and children's mental health and works in her own private practice in the Philadelphia, Pennsylvania, area.

Vincent J. Scotta is a master colorist and hairstylist, currently working with Couleurs Salon in Ft. Lauderdale, Florida. His work has appeared in *Glamour, ELLE,* and *Bride.* Roughly 20 percent of his clients are teenagers. He answers questions at www.vincentj.com.

Elizabeth Freid is a New York City–based celebrity makeup artist. She has worked with a wide range of clients, including Mandy Moore, the Backstreet Boys, and even former President Bill Clinton.

Mary Rodts, R.N., O.N.C., is a board-certified orthopaedic nurse, surgical nursing practitioner, and teacher of surgical nursing at Rush Presbyterian–St. Luke's Medical Center in Chicago, Illinois. She is part of the medical practice Orthopaedics and Scoliosis Ltd. and is assistant professor at Rush College of Nursing. She also is a member of the Spine Universe Editorial Board at SpineUniverse.com.

Lois G. Jovanovic, M.D., F.A.C.E., is director and chief scientific officer at Sansum Medical Research Institute and clinical professor of medicine in the division of endocrinology at the University of Southern California in Los Angeles. She has a special interest in hormones and development.

Neal Kramer, D.P.M., is a podiatrist working with Kramer and Maehrer LLC, part of the Eastern Pennsylvania Health Network, Sacred Heart Hospital, and St. Luke's Hospital in Bethlehem, Pennsylvania. He helps active people of all ages stay on their feet—free of pain.

Harriet S. Mosatche, Ph.D., is a respected online advice columnist at jfg.girlscouts.org (see the Girl Talk link). She is also the director of program development for the Girl Scouts of the U.S.A. and author of *Girls, What's So Bad About Being Good?* and co-author of *Too Old for This, Too Young for That! Your Survival Guide for the Middle-School Years.* Dr. Mosatche is also a Girl Scout leader.

Mary Polce-Lynch, Ph.D., is assistant director at the Center for Counseling and Career Planning at Randolph-Macon College in Ashland, Virginia. She is coauthor of recently published research, "Adolescent Self-Esteem and Gender: Exploring Relations to Sexual Harassment, Body Image, Media Influence, and Emotional Expression," in the *Journal of Youth and Adolescence.* She also is author of *Boy Talk: How You Can Help Your Son Express His Emotions.*

Raymond C. Traver Jr., M.D., is an orthopaedic surgeon with more than twenty-five years of experience treating adolescents with developmental and traumatic orthopaedic conditions. He is editor of www.medicalproductreview.com, counselor to the SUNY Health Science Center, and member of the State of New York, Upstate Medical University Council.

Gail M. Gross, Ed.D., is a nationally recognized expert on child and juvenile education, development, and behavior and an advocate for the interests of children. As the host of the radio show *Let's Talk* and a weekly chat on www.parenthood.com, Dr. Gross helps parents solve a variety of social and emotional problems that are affecting their children.

Amy Middleman, M.D., M.P.H., is a pediatrician in the Texas Children's Adolescent Medicine Clinic at Texas Children's Hospital, the country's largest pediatric hospital. She specializes in adolescent medicine and helps children overcome diseases to live healthier, happier lives.

Jodi Mindell, Ph.D., is a pediatric sleep expert. Dr. Mindell is associate director of the Sleep Disorders Clinic at The Children's Hospital of Philadelphia, and a professor at St. Joseph's University in Philadelphia. She helps children overcome sleep problems so they can get the rest they need to grow up healthy.

Erika Karres, Ed.D., is clinical assistant professor in the school of education at the University of North Carolina in Chapel Hill and author of *Make Your Kids Smarter* and *Violence-Proof Your Kids.* Dr. Karres is an award-winning, nationally recognized educator and expert on school violence.

Index